THE reinvented HOME

THE reinvented HOME

THE reinvented HOME

REUSE
+
RECLAIM
+
RENEW

EMILY HENSON

Photography by Catherine Gratwicke

RYLAND PETERS & SMALL

Senior designer
Megan Smith
Senior commissioning editor
Annabel Morgan
Location research
Jess Walton
Head of production
Patricia Harrington
Creative director
Leslie Harrington

First published as *Create* in 2022.
This edition published in 2026 by
Ryland Peters & Small
20–21 Jockey's Fields,
London, WC1R 4BW

www.rylandpeters.com
Email: euregulations@
rylandpeters.com

10 9 8 7 6 5 4 3 2 1

ISBN 978-1-78879-772-6

A CIP record for this book is available from the British Library.

US Library of Congress CIP data has been applied for.

Printed and bound in China.

The authorised representative in the EEA is
Authorised Rep
Compliance Ltd,
Ground Floor,
71 Lower Baggot Street,
Dublin, D01 P593, Ireland
www.arccompliance.com

MIX
Paper | Supporting responsible forestry
FSC® C106563

Contents

Introduction. 6

Gather: unearthing your style. 8

Discovery. 12
The power of paint. 14
The beauty of the basics. 20
Creative contrast. 28
Reuse/reclaim/reinvent. 34
Make your own. 44

Stories. 50
A modern vintage seaside gem. 52
A playful eco new-build. 62
The old brewery. 72
Not your average beach house. 84
Sustainable lakeside living. 96
A Dutch cabinet of curiosities. 106
The brewery barn. 116
A post office reinvented. 124
Handmade in Bristol. 134
A retro-modern new-build. 142
Loft life in East Berlin. 150
A compact and joyful townhouse. 160

Conscious shopping. 170
Business credits. 171
Picture credits. 172
Acknowledgments. 173
Index. 174

Introduction.

In my previous books, I've written about the idea of creativity before consumption – being resourceful and creative instead of always buying new. In *The Reinvented Home* I focus entirely on this idea of creativity, reinvention and sustainability, not only for the sake of the planet, but also for the joy and satisfaction of creating a truly original home. I recently embarked on my own new (old) house adventure, slowly renovating a bungalow in Margate in between writing the chapters. Visiting the homes featured within these pages has inspired me anew and it gives me great pleasure to share them with you.

I was exposed to the idea of shopping second-hand from a young age – my mum had an antique clothing shop in London and later in Ramsgate. I tagged along to charity shops, jumble sales and Portobello Road Market as she searched for vintage pieces, and spent afternoons parading around her shop in original flapper dresses and 1940s gabardine suits. When I discovered my love for interiors, I was already primed for the thrill of buying second-hand, so mixing new and old came naturally. But I didn't dress or decorate in this way because I cared about the environment – rather, developing my own style through fashion and interiors felt crucial to my self-expression. But now, nearly 40 years after my mum introduced me to the concept of second-hand, shopping like this feels just as crucial for the survival of the planet.

Most of us already have too much. We buy new things, then feel we need more new things to match the other new things we bought. It's an endless cycle that leads to waste. Sustainability has become a bit of a buzzword but the idea of reusing, repurposing and recycling in interiors isn't new – it's how many have decorated for years – but finally it's no longer a niche thing and as a result it's easier than ever to get involved. As an art director and set designer, I've learned to be canny, creative and resourceful when designing shoots, and many of the tricks I've learned translate to home decorating. On these pages you'll see ideas I've used at home as well as many more that I've been inspired to try.

Consuming less and shopping more consciously may be a slower way of decorating, but it is thrilling when you succeed in achieving the look you love while often spending less in the process. Unless you are supporting a small business, an artist or craftsperson, or a manufacturer with proven green credentials, I encourage you to think twice before buying new, and to consider ways to reinvent things you already own rather than replacing them. I think the best way to be sustainable in interiors is to keep things that have already been produced in circulation. If you must buy new, then shop consciously. I appreciate that it isn't always possible to shop in this way, but even small changes add up. Even if you buy furniture from a flat-pack superstore, aim to hold onto it long term rather than treating it as a short-term throwaway solution. And always take the time to sell or give away unwanted items instead of throwing them away. We can all be part of the solution at the same time as creating homes that bear our signature style.

Gather: unearthing your style.

Decorating in a creative and conscious way is one thing, but figuring out the look you love is another one altogether! Many people tell me that they like too many styles and don't know which one to choose, and I often feel exactly the same. I see countless homes, decorated in many varying styles, thanks to my work as an art director, and I love most of them. I might leave a shoot location thinking 'I want white-painted floorboards just like that!'. Then at the next shoot: 'I want colourful patterned tile!'. And later that month at yet another location… 'I want concrete floors!' Being attracted to a wide range of different interiors styles can be paralysing, and many people get stuck at this point, putting off placing a picture on the wall or hanging a curtain for fear of it being 'wrong'. I tackle this challenge in three different ways; two are mindset changes, but the other is more tangible:

Moodboard your way to your signature style.

No doubt you will have heard about using moodboards when developing an interior scheme, but I suggest creating one – either digital or physical – as a tool to explore and develop your own sense of style. You may think that you are drawn to multiple different interior styles, but once you start gathering images you'll find yourself gravitating time and again to a particular look. Seeing images grouped together on the page will help to crystallize what best represents your style. Once you've established this, then it's time to create a moodboard per room. This will detail the look you want to achieve, the items you currently own and plan to reuse or repurpose, and any additional items that need to be sourced. Organizing yourself in this way avoids waste (you can often shop your own home, for example) and sparks creativity.

Decorate slowly.

Once you embrace the mindset of slow decorating, you will find that your style emerges organically over time. Living in a space that is unfinished leaves the door open, allowing inspiration to strike and ideas to evolve. Often, costly mistakes can be avoided by simply taking your time (written from a desk amid the building site that is my new house!).

Forget the myth of the forever home.

If you think of your home as a 'forever home', every decision seems too important to mess up. And this mindset can stunt creativity. If you think this is the last bathroom sink you're ever going to buy, then it has to be absolutely perfect. It has to be THE ONE! And seeking perfection in this way can lead to paralysis. Even if you're confident of your style right now, it's still going to change and evolve over time so allow yourself the freedom to anticipate that, knowing that nothing is forever.

Creating a moodboard.

Simply cut and stick printed inspiration images onto a large piece of card. Or go digital and use Pinterest (@lifeunstyled) to save images, creating categories – floors, kitchens, textiles, etc. Then use a mood board app, Powerpoint or Google Slides to lay out your chosen images, moving them around until it feels right. Remember – it's the process that's important.

WERELDKAART

Discovery.

The power of paint.

Paint is accessible and easily achievable, a tool that anyone can use with zero experience or training and where the impact far outweighs the cost and time spent. Leaving aside the usual coat of paint on the walls, there are myriad ways to update your home using this versatile medium.

First of all, almost anything can be painted. Metal, wood, tile, ceramics, floors, ceilings – there is likely to be a suitable paint product for it. There are many options for paints that are less harmful for both you and the environment (see sources, pages 170–171), but my (admittedly unscientific) opinion is that using any paint to update a piece of furniture that would otherwise get dumped must surely outweigh the negatives.

Some people are opposed to painting wood, whether it's in the shape of furniture, doors or fireplaces. I am not one of those people. I certainly wouldn't suggest coating a classic Ercol chair in high gloss, but there is so much brown furniture out there and charity shops and online marketplaces are brimming with tired wooden chairs and tables of no particularly distinguished origin that can enjoy a whole new life with a lick of paint. Not everyone loves the look of bare wood, and for them there is paint.

I have a few favourite creative updates with paint. Painting old or unattractive radiators the same colour as the walls can make them disappear, while a contrasting colour will make them stand out. Paint internal doors with a pop of colour to make a statement, or link the colour palette of a series of adjoining rooms and hallways, so that the long view tells a story as well the room itself. If you're feeling artistic, think about adding a border where the wall meets the ceiling or paint woodwork/trim a contrasting colour. Paint a panel of colour on the wall to create an interesting backdrop for a piece of art or a shelf. Paint is your go-to for instant impact, whatever your skill level.

Matt and muted. In this dressing room, the walls, floor, fireplace and trim are all coated in Blush by Little Greene, for a luxurious enveloping effect set against the darker shade of the bedroom (above). A cluster of small wooden cabinets painted in rich but muted shades of chalk paint become works of art on chalky painted walls (opposite).

Discovery.

The power of paint.

Paint is accessible and easily achievable, a tool that anyone can use with zero experience or training and where the impact far outweighs the cost and time spent. Leaving aside the usual coat of paint on the walls, there are myriad ways to update your home using this versatile medium.

First of all, almost anything can be painted. Metal, wood, tile, ceramics, floors, ceilings – there is likely to be a suitable paint product for it. There are many options for paints that are less harmful for both you and the environment (see sources, pages 170–171), but my (admittedly unscientific) opinion is that using any paint to update a piece of furniture that would otherwise get dumped must surely outweigh the negatives.

Some people are opposed to painting wood, whether it's in the shape of furniture, doors or fireplaces. I am not one of those people. I certainly wouldn't suggest coating a classic Ercol chair in high gloss, but there is so much brown furniture out there and charity shops and online marketplaces are brimming with tired wooden chairs and tables of no particularly distinguished origin that can enjoy a whole new life with a lick of paint. Not everyone loves the look of bare wood, and for them there is paint.

I have a few favourite creative updates with paint. Painting old or unattractive radiators the same colour as the walls can make them disappear, while a contrasting colour will make them stand out. Paint internal doors with a pop of colour to make a statement, or link the colour palette of a series of adjoining rooms and hallways, so that the long view tells a story as well the room itself. If you're feeling artistic, think about adding a border where the wall meets the ceiling or paint woodwork/trim a contrasting colour. Paint a panel of colour on the wall to create an interesting backdrop for a piece of art or a shelf. Paint is your go-to for instant impact, whatever your skill level.

Matt and muted. In this dressing room, the walls, floor, fireplace and trim are all coated in Blush by Little Greene, for a luxurious enveloping effect set against the darker shade of the bedroom (above). A cluster of small wooden cabinets painted in rich but muted shades of chalk paint become works of art on chalky painted walls (opposite).

Discovery.

The power of paint.

Paint is accessible and easily achievable, a tool that anyone can use with zero experience or training and where the impact far outweighs the cost and time spent. Leaving aside the usual coat of paint on the walls, there are myriad ways to update your home using this versatile medium.

First of all, almost anything can be painted. Metal, wood, tile, ceramics, floors, ceilings – there is likely to be a suitable paint product for it. There are many options for paints that are less harmful for both you and the environment (see sources, pages 170–171), but my (admittedly unscientific) opinion is that using any paint to update a piece of furniture that would otherwise get dumped must surely outweigh the negatives.

Some people are opposed to painting wood, whether it's in the shape of furniture, doors or fireplaces. I am not one of those people. I certainly wouldn't suggest coating a classic Ercol chair in high gloss, but there is so much brown furniture out there and charity shops and online marketplaces are brimming with tired wooden chairs and tables of no particularly distinguished origin that can enjoy a whole new life with a lick of paint. Not everyone loves the look of bare wood, and for them there is paint.

I have a few favourite creative updates with paint. Painting old or unattractive radiators the same colour as the walls can make them disappear, while a contrasting colour will make them stand out. Paint internal doors with a pop of colour to make a statement, or link the colour palette of a series of adjoining rooms and hallways, so that the long view tells a story as well the room itself. If you're feeling artistic, think about adding a border where the wall meets the ceiling or paint woodwork/trim a contrasting colour. Paint a panel of colour on the wall to create an interesting backdrop for a piece of art or a shelf. Paint is your go-to for instant impact, whatever your skill level.

Matt and muted. In this dressing room, the walls, floor, fireplace and trim are all coated in Blush by Little Greene, for a luxurious enveloping effect set against the darker shade of the bedroom (above). A cluster of small wooden cabinets painted in rich but muted shades of chalk paint become works of art on chalky painted walls (opposite).

THE ENGLISH ROSE

Colour wheel. In the Lyon family home (pages 52–62), few surfaces are left unpainted. In the formal sitting room, Farrow & Ball's Hague Blue provides a strong backdrop for Natasha's collection of colourful vintage homewares and upholstery (opposite). In daughter Bea's bedroom, a wooden dresser is painted in a dusty rose to contrast with Little Greene's Yellow-Pink walls (above). In son Thomas's room, a soothing celadon green looks sweet behind the colourful drawers of a reclaimed classroom storage unit (right). The hallway is painted in rich blue tones, with the balustrades in a semi-gloss finish for easier cleaning (above right).

All in the detail. A geometric design is painted on the walls of this high-ceilinged loft space, drawing the eye up to and framing a gallery of artwork (left). A living room door is painted rich egg-yolk yellow, but the door frame has been left unpainted (below left). The same yellow is used on the kitchen door frame just down the hall, linking the two rooms (below). In the kitchen the walls are unpainted plaster, sealed with decorator's varnish, but the skirtings/baseboards are painted pale blue, a band of which runs up the corners of the room and creates the effect of coving/molding where the walls meet the ceiling. A simple trick to help radiators blend in is to paint them the same shade as the wall (opposite).

EJP + JJP FOREVER

The beauty of the basics.

Creative use of basic building materials isn't a new idea, but it is becoming more mainstream. On these pages, you'll see desks and benches built from plywood, bookshelves crafted from cut scaffolding boards and raw plastered walls left unpainted. There are also innovative ideas, like taps/faucets fashioned from copper piping and used in a luxe micro-cemented bathroom and a kitchen island built from water-resistant MDF, a temporary solution that became a permanent one. And there are simple ones too, like updating inexpensive paper globe lanterns with brightly coloured flex and sourcing shelving from catering supply stores. It's all about challenging convention and being steadfast in your conviction of what you find beautiful.

Stop thinking of bare plaster walls as unfinished, and you will see them for what they actually are: a gorgeously textured surface that's far less expensive than Venetian plaster (your plasterer may question your sanity, but that's how you know it's a good idea). Similarly, electrical cables that are usually chased into walls can be surface-mounted in galvanized conduit piping, saving money and adding an industrial edge to any room. When the owner of one of the homes featured in this book asked her builder to fit her electrics in this way, he thought she was mad. Now he's installing them in every house in their village.

I'm a big fan of shopping at catering equipment stores for freestanding commercial kitchen units, shelves and sinks – they're excellent places to look for unconventional yet stylish solutions for the home that are also inexpensive, durable and hygienic. Once a stainless steel trolley is loaded with vintage crockery, it no longer looks like it belongs in a sterile commercial kitchen. And there are more affordable ways of achieving the look of poured or polished concrete floors without blowing the budget. Floor screed is used to level out floors in preparation for wooden floorboards or tile, but more and more people are leaving screed floors uncovered for an industrial look at a fraction of the cost. Again, watch for the horror on your builder's face when you explain that one.

Keep it simple. An oversized paper lantern is an inexpensive but stylish solution to overhead lighting, particularly if you have high ceilings. Add coloured fabric flex to complement or contrast with your interiors (above). Silvery-grey plastered walls are left unpainted for a luxe industrial but cost-saving look (opposite). Depending on the type of plaster, the finish could be pink, grey or cream.

Just peachy. This birch plywood kitchen was designed and built by homeowner Francesca Gaskin and led to the launch of her business Jetsam Made. Plywood doors like these can be added to basic kitchen cabinets and sealed, stained or painted. The gypsum plaster walls with a peachy-pink finish are every bit as beautiful as expensive Venetian plaster but without the hefty price tag.

Heart of the home. This kitchen island with integrated hob was built from green water-resistant MDF and was intended as a temporary solution until a 'proper' kitchen was fitted (above left). Years on, it is still much loved and hasn't been replaced. In this Dutch kitchen, an industrial-style metal trolley sits within easy reach of the dining table and holds stacks of vintage servewear (above). In another Dutch kitchen, a basic IKEA kitchen was brought to life with a concrete worktop and a vibrant terracotta pink zellige tile splashback (left).

Understated details. In this former post office sorting depot, the original tiled walls were revealed by scraping off layers of bright green paint in what is now the main bedroom (above left). The walls were plastered and left unpainted and the ceiling was left as found. Rather than going to the expense of embedding cables in the walls, the electrical wiring was surface mounted in galvanized conduit. Instead of a traditional handrail, a cavity was cut into the wall, its edge polished smooth for a comfortable grip (above right). More galvanized metal conduit, here connecting to a vintage ceramic wall-mounted bulb holder (above right). In a newly built Dutch home, the stairs were kept very simple with chunky ply, lightly whitewashed and sealed (right).

Use every inch.

In this home, space has been maximized by building a pantry under the stairs, tucked behind this door. In addition to the internal shelves, MDF cubbies were added to the exterior walls, holding books on the living room side and jars of decanted dried goods in the kitchen area.

I love you
MAGGIE DENT
THE FOUNTAINHEAD
Marshall
The Fran Lebowitz Reader

Clever zoning. When you enter this Dutch home, you are greeted with a practical and attractive coat rack and storage unit built from plywood. Occupying the rear of the kitchen wall, it is an efficient use of dead space. Woven baskets help to organize hats, scarves and shoes and add warmth and texture.

Shelve it. Floor-to-ceiling shelves made from scaffolding boards hang in the corner of this bedroom, allowing easy access to bedtime reading material (opposite). The metal end bands all face outwards for a uniform finish. Scaffolding boards can be sourced second hand via online marketplaces or bought new from builder's merchants. Because they are chunky, make sure to use heavy-duty shelf brackets firmly anchored to the walls. Sturdy metal wire shelving – the kind often seen in restaurant kitchens – works well in this pantry (above). Napkins, tablecloths and other kitchen miscellanea are stored in colourful plastic vegetable crates of the type often thrown out by corner shops.

Creative contrast.

Some of the most memorable homes I've visited over the years are those with a playful approach to contrast, coupling new with old, handmade and chain store, pops of colour set against neutrals. It's experimental and intriguing and personal – all of the things I love! I've written about using contrast in my previous books but, like all my favourite ideas, it bears revisiting.

Creating contrast through an unexpected mix of colours, eras, patterns and materials brings a home to life in a way that little else can. Without contrast, a home can feel flat and lifeless. It can be as simple as the addition of a brightly coloured lampshade to an otherwise neutral room, or a splashback of textured pink Moroccan zellige tile next to a shiny stainless-steel sink; a bold painting in an ornate gilt frame hung on an unpainted plaster wall, or a glossy tomato-red fridge against a chalky black wall.

Thinking about contrast is also helpful when trying to decorate in a more conscious way. I appreciate that it's difficult for everyone to fully commit to buying second hand or spending more on independent designers who use sustainable materials and methods. Supplementing new pieces with some reclaimed or repurposed items is better than doing nothing. It's not easy to stop consuming new things completely, or to always consume consciously, but small changes are better than none. And contrast between old and new never goes out of style.

Decorating in this way allows a huge amount of freedom. Freedom to buy that random vintage sculpture at a charity shop because you know it will look brilliant on your modern box shelf. Freedom to put a too-small lampshade on a too-big lamp, just because you like the way it looks. Freedom to hang a lilac sink on a mint-green tiled wall purely because you're bored of ubiquitous white metro-tiled bathrooms. Our homes are the one place where we can freely express ourselves, our creativity, our ingenuity, without fear of judgement – so get mixing!

Negative space. This bedroom works visually because the abundant different patterns share a common colour story and are grounded by the white bedspread and floors (above). Similarly, in this kitchen/dining area textured metal walls and patterned tile are broken up by the plain painted tabletop and green cabinets (opposite).

NOW

Challenge your expectations. A much larger lampshade would have been the obvious choice, but topping this bulbous base with a petite shade looks far more interesting (left). Notice how the red and white stripe is repeated in the framed photo. A small vintage sink was sourced for this tiny lavatory and, keen to avoid the typical monochrome bathroom, the homeowner teamed it with a vibrant magenta tile (below left). A cornflower blue sideboard by Tylko (who source sustainably grown wood for their plywood furniture) contrasts with the terrazzo-style floor in a rented loft (below). Two teenage sisters share this vintage dressing table. They each have a locker-style wardrobe, which gives the room a contemporary edge (opposite).

UPTOWN
LOCAL
GRAND
CENTRAL

Colour contrast. A unique blend of old and new and muted and vibrant delights the eye in this open-plan home. The eclectic mix of furniture is balanced out by a white floor and calming shades of green and blue paint.

Use every inch.

In this child's room, a single bed was built into the the eaves with a cupboard squeezed in alongside (right). The unit was clad in reclaimed boards and decorated with earthy chalk paint. The sleek lines of the bold red table contrast beautifully with the rougher wood.

Reuse/reclaim/ reinvent.

The idea of repurposing something for the home may not be new, but it is more important than ever before. Not least because it keeps in use and in circulation items that would otherwise go to landfill. It's all about creating less waste.

Another reason – the icing on the cake, if you will – is that your home will be uniquely yours. It will be filled with pieces with history. You'll be able to share stories about where an item came from and how you adapted it and the satisfaction will be immense. It can be as simple as buying a second-hand lamp base instead of a new one and adding a different shade, or throwing a linen sheet over a worn sofa instead of replacing it. Alternatively, it might be as time-consuming as sourcing reclaimed wooden floorboards and refinishing them to fit your home, or adapting an old luggage rack into a pot holder.

There are a couple of things that put people off the idea of reuse or reclaimation. First is the assumption that it's only relevant if you're into vintage or retro styles. But with so many online marketplaces out there, people will buy and sell almost anything, and nearly-new contemporary pieces can be found for bargain prices. Imagine the scenario: somebody buys a new luxury bathtub only to find that it doesn't fit, but they can't return it. Someone else orders far more floor tiles than they need, and the surplus are up for grabs at a fraction of their original price.

Secondly, there is a level of patience and flexibility required to decorate in this way, and it won't suit everyone. You have to be open to decorating slowly as it will likely take longer to find what you have in mind, which can prove frustrating. On the flipside, you may go in search of one thing but end up with something else that you were looking for – when I was hunting for salvaged wood flooring, I came home with a mint-green 1930s bathroom sink instead. The sink helped me out of my 'too much choice' paralysis (I know you've been there) and set in motion the design of the rest of the bathroom, but I'm still looking for flooring... If you're up for seeing decorating as an ongoing and creative game that you're always playing, your prize will be a home that cannot be replicated.

A kitchen with soul. Everything you see in this kitchen is second hand except the appliances (above and right). A tall metal trolley houses a rotating group of plants, its wheels making it easy to move to sunnier spots when needed. Above a stripped pine cabinet now used as a kitchen island hangs an old luggage rack reclaimed from a train and converted into a pot hanging rack.

It's all wood. In this beach-house bedroom, the walls are clad in old wooden boards. The headboard was topped with a piece of wood to create a slim shelf (left). Walls are covered in rusted metal sheeting while doors are clad with wood from old potato crates (opposite above). The artwork is from nowbepresent.com. Potato-crate wood also features in the bathroom (opposite below right). A patchwork of salvaged boards works when larger quantities are hard to source (opposite below left).

NOW

Creative DIY.

Rather than opting for bland modern MDF wardrobe/closet doors, three pairs of reclaimed double doors have been sourced, stripped and fitted to create a wall of storage that is an intriguing feature rather than a dull necessity.

Brick by brick, tile by tile. In this cavernous room, a brick wall stretches up to the vaulted roof (page 38). The owners source second-hand furniture and recycled building materials whenever possible, with the occasional design classic added to the mix. The mantelpiece was a gift from the husband's father, a former antiques dealer. In this kitchen, handmade tiles by Emery & Cie line the walls and a new window frame is softened by the simple trick of adding a length of reclaimed timber within the frame (page 39).

Second time around. This vast home exclusively uses vintage and antique finds, from the furniture to the picture frames (above). A vintage glazed metal medicine cabinet allows its stylist owner to display all her prettiest possessions (right). In the home studio of a jewellery designer, a specially designed desk was constructed from offcuts of plywood (opposite). The electric blue carpet was reused after being ripped out of a project the couple had worked on years before.

Creative DIY.

Rather than opting for bland modern MDF wardrobe/closet doors, three pairs of reclaimed double doors have been sourced, stripped and fitted to create a wall of storage that is an intriguing feature rather than a dull necessity.

STAY
BLACK
STAY
HOMIE

Rustic elegance. In this old brewery, the ceilings were stripped out to reveal steel beams and the original old air bricks that were used for drying hops (opposite above). Pieces of reclaimed timber were used to patch any gaps and the simplicity of the wire pendant means it does not distract from the aged beauty of the ceiling. The original tile in what was once the staff room of a postal sorting depot now gleams after refinishing. A band of black paint was added to the wall in the guest bedroom and vintage brass coat hangers were fixed to the tile (opposite below).

Make your own.

I was hesitant about including this section, because a lot of people tell me they aren't creative or skilled or patient enough to make anything. But if you picked up this particular book, you must have a creative inclination; otherwise it wouldn't have piqued your interest. And anyone with even a tiny dash of creativity combined with enthusiasm and willingness to learn (and to make mistakes) can add an element of the handmade to their home.

Contributing to the decoration of a room by creating with your own hands is a deeply satisfying process. You also get to be that smug person who tells guests, 'Oh that? I just whipped it up in my spare time.' (Even if it actually took many months of blood, sweat and tears.) Joking aside, making something yourself is putting your signature on your home and it gives you a deeper appreciation for decorative objects when you've spent time and energy on their creation.

Once you start to really see objects for what they are, making them doesn't seem quite as daunting. After all, what is a headboard? In its simplest form, it's just a piece of wood with foam and fabric stapled in place and propped up behind a bed. What is a curtain? It can be as simple as a length of material (like a tablecloth or pretty fringed hammam towel) hung from a pole with no-sew clips. And a stair runner? It could be shorter lengths of vintage rugs or runners stitched or pieced together. Not all the projects seen in these pages are beginner level, and some do require sewing or carpentry skills, but I urge you to think about what you would enjoy making and challenge yourself to learn.

Alternatively, you could be the designer and hire an expert to help with the making. A friend recently commissioned a joiner to make the most beautiful dining table for a fraction of the cost of a similar one bought new. She didn't saw, plane or polish the wood herself, but she poured creativity into its design nonetheless. I don't want to simplify things, because making can be difficult and mistakes will be made, especially when learning something new. But in my opinion, a slightly wonky cushion sewn by you beats a perfect one also owned by many others.

The final flourish. To disguise a kitchen extractor hood, a surround was built with an integral shelf for plants (faux, to withstand the heat). Finished with plaster and a strip of unpainted timber, it blends right in (above). Wool/yarn collected by the owner and used as inspiration for her home's colour story was later used to create this large pendant by carefully winding lengths of the wool around a large metal frame (opposite).

beschuit
Hille
Zaandam

Elevate the ordinary. A pair of mismatched lace tablecloths make lovely curtains where you want some light to filter through and don't require privacy. Hung from bamboo poles by curtain rings that were pushed through the fabric, it couldn't be simpler (opposite). A bathroom tap/faucet was fashioned out of copper piping and brass outdoor taps, a surprisingly simple project (above left). In this kitchen/diner, the table and the bench seating were handmade by the resourceful and creative owner (left). Seating like this allows more people to squeeze around a table and offers additional storage space if the lids are hinged. Wooden pallets have been used to build this low-slung sofa, topped with large chunky floor cushions in embroidered fabrics (above).

Creative DIY.

This hanging rail does double duty, both screening a bedroom area in an open-plan loft and providing clothes storage. The sturdy wooden dowel is fixed by thick chain to the ceiling. For a secure hold, hooks should be drilled into ceiling joists or use ceiling anchors/toggle bolts that are strong enough to bear the load.

Tactile textiles. These square floor cushions covered in a variety of Dutch wax fabrics were made by the homeowner (above). If you can't sew, you could outsource a project like this to a local seamstress or tailor. Many advertise online and making cushion covers may cost less than you think. This headboard was made by its owner from vintage Indian fabric found in Paris (opposite). Once the wooden base of a DIY headboard has been cut to shape and a layer of foam has been added, a piece of fabric can simply be wrapped round it and stapled to the back.

Stories.

WHO *Natasha and John Lyon, Bea (6), Thomas (4) and cats Cheddar and Milo.*
WHAT *A semi-detached six-bedroom Edwardian house, 260 sq.m/2798 sq.ft.*
WHERE *Margate, Kent.*

A modern vintage seaside gem.

MORE THAN JUST A HOUSE
SOTTSASS
FLOWER
The Flower Fix
Wreaths

Natasha and John Lyon seem to have an instinct for buying property in up-and-coming areas before anyone (even they) realize that they're up and coming. They've progressed from a two-bedroom flat in a now-fashionable part of North London to a four-bedroom house in a newly desirable part of East London to this impressive six-bedroom family home in Margate, quickly becoming the coolest coastal town on the Kent coast.

For 15 years Natasha was a handbag designer for well-known luxury brands – a job that allowed her to travel extensively, picking up interiors inspiration along the way. She and John bought this house more than three years ago and initially tackled the less-exciting jobs – treating damp and fixing the roof and chimneys. They were lucky that the house already had a large kitchen extension. Knowing that much of the space could be updated cosmetically, and relying on Natasha's talent for styling her many vintage furnishings and accessories, the couple decided the kitchen was where they would spend their money. John is a keen cook, so a well-functioning kitchen is important to him. After extensive research on kitchens from high to low price points and everything in between, they chose to work with a local joiner who built a bespoke kitchen to meet John's culinary requirements. They sold the existing kitchen on Facebook Marketplace and are planning on reusing the slate floor tiles for the garden patio.

When the pandemic hit and work came to a standstill, the couple decided to collaborate on a new business – Appreciation Project, an online sustainable dried flower delivery and homeware brand. Natasha runs the creative side and John advises on operations while also working in technology sales. Natasha has set up a home studio in the attic, filled with dried bouquets and branded packaging yet also oozing style, thanks to her decision to paint the room a rich shade of green. Throughout the house, colour plays a starring role, with every room except the kitchen painted in bold hues. In fact, there was so much painting to be done that it took nine months to complete! Nothing was safe from the painter's brush, and the result is a captivating palette from top to bottom.

Aside from the kitchen and armchairs and sofas (which were bought new from Sofa.com), pretty much everything is second-hand. Natasha is dedicated to vintage and has a few favourite haunts aside from the usual online sources.

While there's no strict colour scheme for the home as a whole – something that I entirely approve of – a splash of red pops up in almost every room. Sometimes that's all you need to create a link throughout an interior – a small pop here and there. The Lyons have created a joyous home, lived-in and relaxed yet filled with mementoes that tell their story.

A room to bloom. In Natasha's home office (opposite), bundles of dried flowers and stacks of boxes sit on painted wooden floorboards. The walls and ceilings are enveloped in the same rich green, Jungle Fever 1 by Dulux. The hallway (page 52) has original parquet flooring and a rich combination of paint colours; the paler shade is Oval Room Blue while the darker one is De Nimes, both from Farrow & Ball. In the sitting room (page 53) the wall and shelf are painted in Farrow & Ball's Hague Blue.

Dark and moody. In the family bathroom (above), the blingy tub was already in place. Natasha brought it into line with her style by adding an eclectic and colourful collection of furniture and textiles. The wooden cabinet was painted red and adapted to hold a sink, while the striped curtain is a piece of fabric pinned onto a pole. The blue walls are Little Greene's Brighton. In the main bedroom (left, above left and opposite) the walls are painted in Myland's Borough Market as are the fireplace and the shelf. On the bed, Natasha has deftly mixed patterns and colours, with stripes playing a key role. A piece of unhemmed striped fabric has been draped over a side table; a simple trick that can be used to jazz up small tables in any room. Rather than reupholstering the round chair cushion, Natasha covered it with throws (opposite).

When to splurge.

There are times when you may need or choose to invest in something new, as was the case in this kitchen. John is a keen cook and the open kitchen/dining room is the family hub. The old units were removed and sold online, and a local joiner was hired to build new cabinets, including this large island, topped with robust stainless steel and painted in Little Greene's Olive.

Dark and moody. In the family bathroom (above), the blingy tub was already in place. Natasha brought it into line with her style by adding an eclectic and colourful collection of furniture and textiles. The wooden cabinet was painted red and adapted to hold a sink, while the striped curtain is a piece of fabric pinned onto a pole. The blue walls are Little Greene's Brighton. In the main bedroom (left, above left and opposite) the walls are painted in Myland's Borough Market as are the fireplace and the shelf. On the bed, Natasha has deftly mixed patterns and colours, with stripes playing a key role. A piece of unhemmed striped fabric has been draped over a side table; a simple trick that can be used to jazz up small tables in any room. Rather than reupholstering the round chair cushion, Natasha covered it with throws (opposite).

BALSAMIC
VINEGAR
SEL
Edmond Fallot

BRITISH
SEA-
FISHERMEN
PETER F. ANSON
The New Creative Home
The Selby Is in Your Place

Colour clash. Daughter Bea's room was transformed with a luscious clash of colours. The interior is mustard (Yellow-Pink by Little Greene) and dusty rose, and the open door gives a glimpse of zingy colour in her brother's room next door. The hallway side of the door is De Nimes by Farrow & Ball, while Thomas's room is Japanese Maze 2 by Dulux. The stair runner was created by piecing together vintage rugs (opposite).

Q&A

5 minutes with Natasha & John.

What's the most important thing for you at home?
It's important our home is full of creativity; things to feed the eyes and the imagination. I want this for my kids, for them to grow up around interesting art and books. It's also important for me – as a designer, I want to be surrounded by objects, textures and colours that inspire me.

Do you have a decorating/design philosophy?
Colour! Don't be afraid to use it. My take on design is eclectic – each room is filled with special pieces that have a story to go with them. I divide large rooms into 'zones' and accessorize each one individually, layering cushions, blankets, side tables, lamps and books. Soon the room starts to feel very cosy and is filled with lots of detail. I will never be a minimalist, because I'm obsessed with colours, textures and objects.

Describe a creative solution to a challenge you faced with your home.
When I get bored of a piece of furniture but can't afford or find anything to replace it, I cover it in fabric. I did this to the bedside tables/nightstands in our bedroom and to a coffee table in the family room. It changes the space immediately.

Where do you shop for your home? Do you have a favourite store or source?
We have always bought sofas and chairs from Sofa.com, the quality is brilliant. In Norwich we stumbled across the most incredible shop called Vintage Mischief; we have bought a lot from them over the years. I also have a few treasures from Vantage Living, including the wicker elephants and the glass coffee table in the front lounge.

Do you tend to stay in one property for a long time or do you prefer to move or reinvent your home frequently?
This is our third property and we have stayed in each one thinking we will be there longer than we have been. However, this home is different, it is a true family home. There is a lot of space and it can evolve; already it has taken on an office for John and my office has adapted into a studio for Appreciation Project. I can see other rooms changing over time into a library/homework room and the boot room becoming a utility room. There is also a loft space and three rooms in the cellar. Because there is still lots left to do combined with the fact we can grow into the house we will be here for a long time yet. However, I'm sure there will come a point where I will want to flex my creative interior desires once again.

What's next for your home?
The next project is the family bathroom, a shower room and reinstating a toilet next to the kids' bedroom that had been removed. We're also keen to put stained glass into the front door and surrounding windows.

A playful eco new-build.

WHO *Jet van der Graaf and Michiel Roos, sons Roemer (12) and Rein (10), and puppy Vlok.*
WHAT *A newly-built two-storey townhouse, 96 sq.m/1033 sq.ft.*
WHERE *'s-Hertogenbosch, The Netherlands.*

anton corbijn
GEMEENTE MUSEUM DEN HAAG

I may sound like I'm romanticizing here, but when we visited this newly-built community of 24 houses, a trio of ducks (all with names) roamed the communal gardens, countless children wandered in the back door asking if the kids could come out to play and neighbours chatted as they worked in their gardens. Although within walking distance of the city's central train station, this community feels like a little bubble of tranquillity amid the chaos of city life. It was designed, developed and built by its residents, a group of people including Jet and Michiel, who pooled their resources, found architects and builders and dreamed up the community in which they wanted to live.

The houses vary in size and style but are all ecologically sensitive and sustainably built, mainly from wood. They are constructed around a communal area, with each small private garden backing onto a larger space for all to use (including the resident ducks). Residents also designed a community building; essentially a large greenhouse with a kitchen that's available for parties, movie nights and other gatherings.

Jet and Michiel, a graphic designer and software architect respectively, were able to design their home exactly as they wanted, adapting plans to suit their budget and lifestyle. Jet occasionally works in interior design and was excited to use her skills on their new home. They opted for a mostly open-plan interior, with the ground floor opening up to the second where mezzanine-style sleeping floors, as Jet calls them, have been added. This doesn't offer a lot of privacy – the bathrooms being the only rooms with proper doors – but it suits the family. The footprint of the house isn't large, but by keeping everything open and with long sight lines they have maximized the available space and created a playful and unique layout. 'Think in height, not just in width and depth,' Jet offers.

When the couple got the keys, there was still much to be done – plastering and painting, building a staircase to the sleeping floors, treating the raw wood surfaces with linseed oil, and finishing the kitchen and bathrooms. For weeks friends brought them dinner as they did a spot of indoor camping while completing the work. The wood-burning stove arrived just in time for the cold winter, and it was this piece that made the house feel like home.

Clever use of space is key here, with a larder slotted in under the staircase and bookshelves added to its exterior (see page 25). Much of the interior is clad in various plywoods, with the newly installed beams left exposed and unpainted. In keeping with the family's sustainable lifestyle, most of the furnishings are second hand, collected over the years or made by artist friends, and make a characterful juxtaposition to the raw finishes of the interior.

Open-plan living. The stylish and hard-working wood burner sits beside the living-room nook. The walls are painted in Noa from sustainable paint brand Fairf (pages 62–63). Looking up from the back windows of the ground floor, Jet's office above is clearly visible (opposite). The decision to keep everything open plan with few walls and doors has created a unique, playful layout in this family home. Just seen above Jet's desk is the floor of the mezzanine level above, which was constructed to house the sleeping platforms.

Clever zoning.

A half-height wall was built to create a sense of separation between the dining area and the kitchen. This has the added benefit of creating additional space for much-needed cabinets and other storage in the kitchen. The wall hides much of the inevitable clutter but allows whoever is cooking to engage with what's happening in the dining and living areas.

Kitchen details. The dining table was built from scaffolding poles and chunky lengths of timber and hanging above it are pendants made by designer friends. The blue-green wall paint is Luana by Fairf (above). The back wall of the kitchen is painted in chalkboard paint, a convenient way to keep track of the grocery shopping list (right and opposite). The kitchen units are from IKEA, their practical simplicity elevated by collections of vintage and handmade homeware. Black metal shelves display beautiful china and a lamp with a decorative shade adds a soft glow to the eclectic kitchen (above right).

yoghurt
gember
ROEMAR
KOFFIEBRANDERIJ
KOFFIE
SWEDISH
dill
pickles
Vermicelle
Farine
Chicorée
Sucre
Thym
Laurier
Epices
Girofle
Poivre
Thé
Café

Garden views. Jet's desk was built from plywood offcuts and has a view of the living room below and the gardens behind (below). The spiral staircase (just seen) leads up to the couple's bedroom. In the family bathroom, a skylight allows light to flood in, highlighting the matt black tiles. The side of the bathtub is a sheet of oiled plywood and the wallpaper is by Cole & Son (above right and right). Just to the right as you enter the bathroom is a tiny sink set onto a wooden dresser that was once the children's changing table.

A head for heights. From the upper hallway you can see the sleeping floor above, which makes excellent use of the double-height ceiling. To the right is Jet's office and to the left is the couple's wardrobe with hanging rails plus a vintage screen for privacy. The green walls are painted with Cardamom Skin by Vestingh.

Use every inch.

The boys share a sleeping loft that's tucked into the roof, with windows on both sides for good ventilation. Built above the hallway with stairs leading down to the playroom, this clever idea was a way of gaining more space in a house with a small footprint.

Q&A

5 minutes with Jet & Michiel.

What's the most important thing for you at home?
The dynamics of the spaces match our family; the house is built around us instead of us having to adapt to existing spaces and volumes. Because we were able to design it ourselves, it fits perfectly.

Do you have a decorating/design philosophy?
If you like something because it means something to you then it fits, always. Tell your story, embrace your individuality – that makes it your home.

Describe a creative solution to a challenge you faced with your home.
One of the nicest creative solutions are the windows in the children's bedrooms. We all sleep under the roof and to ensure the flow of fresh air, we made hatches for the boys' room. It looks like they are sleeping in a tree house.

Where do you shop for your home? Do you have a favourite store or source?
I don't actually shop very often for our house; most stuff we have collected over the years. A lot comes from our travels, heirlooms and second-hand finds. Sometimes I invest in a design item, also preferably second hand. We also like unique items, such as the lamps that hang above the table, which were made by artist friends.

Do you prefer to stay in one property for a long time or do you like to move or reinvent your home frequently?
We are not frequent movers, but after around five years new wishes and dreams arise. I would really like to make a big move abroad – more nature and more land around the house.

Is there any other work you're planning to do?
We still have to paint the skirtings/baseboards, but that's not a chore I really want to do! I would also like to replace the kitchen cabinet doors with solid wood fronts, preferably oak.

Floating in the clouds. Jet and Michiel's bedroom is lined with birch plywood sheets, creating a cosy space tucked away high in the eaves with just enough room for a bed and some built-in storage. The room is open to the level below, which prevents the space from feeling claustrophobic. While the lack of privacy may not suit everyone, in this home it works perfectly.

The old brewery.

WHO *Misty Buckley, Reggie Matheson, their children Indiana (10) and Dusty-Rose (9) and cats Biffy and Berry.*
WHAT *The Storehouse, an old brewery dating to 1870, 258 sq.m/2777 sq.ft.*
WHERE *Pilton, Somerset.*

Q&A

5 minutes with Jet & Michiel.

What's the most important thing for you at home?
The dynamics of the spaces match our family; the house is built around us instead of us having to adapt to existing spaces and volumes. Because we were able to design it ourselves, it fits perfectly.

Do you have a decorating/design philosophy?
If you like something because it means something to you then it fits, always. Tell your story, embrace your individuality – that makes it your home.

Describe a creative solution to a challenge you faced with your home.
One of the nicest creative solutions are the windows in the children's bedrooms. We all sleep under the roof and to ensure the flow of fresh air, we made hatches for the boys' room. It looks like they are sleeping in a tree house.

Where do you shop for your home? Do you have a favourite store or source?
I don't actually shop very often for our house; most stuff we have collected over the years. A lot comes from our travels, heirlooms and second-hand finds. Sometimes I invest in a design item, also preferably second hand. We also like unique items, such as the lamps that hang above the table, which were made by artist friends.

Do you prefer to stay in one property for a long time or do you like to move or reinvent your home frequently?
We are not frequent movers, but after around five years new wishes and dreams arise. I would really like to make a big move abroad – more nature and more land around the house.

Is there any other work you're planning to do?
We still have to paint the skirtings/baseboards, but that's not a chore I really want to do! I would also like to replace the kitchen cabinet doors with solid wood fronts, preferably oak.

Floating in the clouds. Jet and Michiel's bedroom is lined with birch plywood sheets, creating a cosy space tucked away high in the eaves with just enough room for a bed and some built-in storage. The room is open to the level below, which prevents the space from feeling claustrophobic. While the lack of privacy may not suit everyone, in this home it works perfectly.

The old brewery.

WHO *Misty Buckley, Reggie Matheson, their children Indiana (10) and Dusty-Rose (9) and cats Biffy and Berry.*
WHAT *The Storehouse, an old brewery dating to 1870, 258 sq.m/2777 sq.ft.*
WHERE *Pilton, Somerset.*

Q&A

5 minutes with Jet & Michiel.

What's the most important thing for you at home?
The dynamics of the spaces match our family; the house is built around us instead of us having to adapt to existing spaces and volumes. Because we were able to design it ourselves, it fits perfectly.

Do you have a decorating/design philosophy?
If you like something because it means something to you then it fits, always. Tell your story, embrace your individuality – that makes it your home.

Describe a creative solution to a challenge you faced with your home.
One of the nicest creative solutions are the windows in the children's bedrooms. We all sleep under the roof and to ensure the flow of fresh air, we made hatches for the boys' room. It looks like they are sleeping in a tree house.

Where do you shop for your home? Do you have a favourite store or source?
I don't actually shop very often for our house; most stuff we have collected over the years. A lot comes from our travels, heirlooms and second-hand finds. Sometimes I invest in a design item, also preferably second hand. We also like unique items, such as the lamps that hang above the table, which were made by artist friends.

Do you prefer to stay in one property for a long time or do you like to move or reinvent your home frequently?
We are not frequent movers, but after around five years new wishes and dreams arise. I would really like to make a big move abroad – more nature and more land around the house.

Is there any other work you're planning to do?
We still have to paint the skirtings/baseboards, but that's not a chore I really want to do! I would also like to replace the kitchen cabinet doors with solid wood fronts, preferably oak.

Floating in the clouds. Jet and Michiel's bedroom is lined with birch plywood sheets, creating a cosy space tucked away high in the eaves with just enough room for a bed and some built-in storage. The room is open to the level below, which prevents the space from feeling claustrophobic. While the lack of privacy may not suit everyone, in this home it works perfectly.

WHO *Misty Buckley, Reggie Matheson, their children Indiana (10) and Dusty-Rose (9) and cats Biffy and Berry.*
WHAT *The Storehouse, an old brewery dating to 1870, 258 sq.m/2777 sq.ft.*
WHERE *Pilton, Somerset.*

The old brewery.

Not many people can claim that their kitchen island was made by the same person who built the pyramid stage at Glastonbury Festival, but for designers Misty and Reggie, who live in the village where the festival takes place and also work on some elements of its design, this is nothing unusual. Together they run a design company with Misty the production designer for tours, music shows and live events, and a client list that includes Coldplay, Stormzy, the Grammy Awards and The Park at Glastonbury Festival.

When they first viewed the property in 2015, the couple were living in a tiny cottage in the same village and were desperate for more space. The former brewery had been made into a residence in the 1970s and at first glance seemed quite unassuming. It wasn't until they pulled down the loft ladder and saw the scale of the attic space that they understood its potential. An experienced designer with an excellent understanding of spatial design, Misty had a clear vision of how the building could look and drew up the plans herself without the help of an architect. The day they got the keys, a friend and colleague from the festival came by for a cup of tea, sledgehammer in hand, and helped bring down partition walls and suspended ceilings, revealing incredible steel columns and beams.

This sense of community involvement would continue throughout the 14 months of the renovations, with Misty and Reggie drawing on a pool of talented colleagues and friends, many of whom work in set construction as builders, welders, joiners and scenic painters. Everyone they know has played a part in bringing the building back to life. Once the couple began to strip it back, they saw an opportunity to restore the old brewery to its original form and decided to take down every floor, ceiling and internal wall and start from scratch. Once they had the shell of the building, they began to put it back together again, careful to keep original elements where possible, including the airbrick ceiling in what is now the living room, once used for drying hops. They scoured reclamation yards, flea markets, skips/dumpsters and auction rooms to source every single element, from floors to doors to sinks to kitchen counters.

When Misty left university, she made a conscious decision to rid her home of flatpack furniture, deciding that instead she would take her time to find exactly what she wanted rather than rushing to fill a gap with something cheap or convenient. This usually means shopping second hand and adapting things where necessary. Every item here has a story, whether it's the beautiful vintage kitchen sink found while working in America and transported home on a production crew lorry, or the kitchen sideboard/cabinet discovered in the north of England and and topped with a zinc worktop. It is this dedication to finding furnishings and materials with a history that gives this home its sense of authenticity. It looks fresh and modern, but also like it's always been there.

Studio space. Misty and Reggie made a home office in the attic, an unexpectedly expansive space. The floors are made from reclaimed boards and the walls are lined with an old wooden plan chest and industrial shelves filled with miniatures of sets that Misty has designed. In the home's entrance (pages 72 and 73) the space was completely reconfigured and an internal window was installed to allow more light into the kitchen.

YOU MAKE ME
ROOMS
tpi

Clever zoning.

The long, narrow sideboard and farmhouse dining table are positioned in parallel to clearly mark out the dining area of the large open-plan living space. Hanging a row of vintage pendant lights above the table also helps to delineate the eating area.

SEIKO

Use every inch.

Narrow offcuts of wood used elsewhere in the refurbishment have been hung on sturdy metal brackets behind the kitchen door. What could have been dead space has instead been put to good use as storage, making items that are in high rotation readily available.

Natural palette. White-painted cabinets, warm wood tones and silvery-grey toned metals are recurrent elements that unify the space (this page and opposite). The large cabinet was found at an antiques market and was topped with a sheet of zinc (opposite). Misty found the large vintage sink in the US and had it shipped home, where it now sits on a piece of reclaimed marble (above right and right, just seen). This variety in materials adds character to the space and the consistently natural palette ties it all together.

Smooth finish. The concrete floors were installed by a friend who was more accustomed to pouring floors for dairy farms than homes, and at a fraction of the cost of residential concrete flooring. The steel beams and post were revealed after the initial demolition.

Perfect patination. Just as with the rest of the house, for the family bathroom Misty and Reggie sourced vintage sanitaryware, taps/faucets and storage to suit their characterful design story and preferred muted palette. Almost everything here has a natural patina and beautiful signs of age or wear, from the reclaimed wooden planks that line the walls to the metal cabinet with its tattered mesh door and the scuffed paint of the shelves that hold towels and toiletries (above, above left and opposite). Against the fresh white walls, even the gilt mirror with its chipped frame tells a story. Only the glossy white tiles and the newly painted sides of the bathtub offer a contrast, and it is this contrast throughout that makes it work (left).

Q&A

5 minutes with Misty & Reggie.

What's the most important thing for you at home?
I love serenity. I love a tidy house – I find it incredibly calming. Having two kids and pets makes it more challenging, but I am pretty disciplined about tidying up before going to bed so in the morning it feels peaceful.

Do you have a decorating/design philosophy?
Simple and natural. I love a restrained colour palette. In my day job, I work with a huge amount of colour in the set, screen content, lighting and visuals. It's colourful, loud, intense yet very creative. My nature is quieter and more reflective, and I think my home echoes my personality more than my job does!

Describe one of your favourite creative solutions to a challenge you faced with your home?
I had always dreamed of a concrete floor but when I looked into it, it was prohibitively expensive. When we heard that a friend had just finished pouring the concrete floor for the milking parlour at a nearby dairy farm, we went and had a look and it was perfect – industrial and matt grey. We asked the contractor if he would consider pouring a concrete floor in our house. He thought we were mad to want industrial flooring in our house and agreed to do it for an extremely reasonable price. I love it so much – it's so warm and smooth. I even love the little fissures and imperfections.

Where do you shop for your home? Do you have a favourite store or source?
Mostly reclamation yards or markets. I know it's a cliché, but I just love rummaging around for a great little pot or jar. I have an obsession with ceramics so I am always on the lookout for a handmade bowl or Japanese coffee cup. There are some incredible potters on Instagram too. In my alternative life I would be a sculptor or a potter.

Do you prefer to stay in one property for a long time or do you like to move or reinvent your home frequently?
I love this house so much. I am always looking online at properties, but nothing has sparked as much interest or inspiration in me as this one. Sometimes I wish I could transport it to my home town (London) or sunny California, as I really crave the city, but I also love it here and I have some beautiful friends in Somerset. I love the light that pours in even on a miserable day, and the variation of the scale from room to room. I am always looking for a project though, so when the barn next door came up for sale, that was the dream situation (see pages 116–123)!

Is there any other work you're planning to do?
I would love to do something with the garden, but it needs to be low maintenance. The idea of weeding fills me with dread – I think about all the other things I could be making in that time!

Not your average beach house.

WHO *Anna and James Carver, their children Finlay (20) and Bodie (13), cats Kogie and Cypher and sometimes James' daughter Minnie (30).*
WHAT *A 1980s bungalow, 130 sq.m/1400 sq.ft.*
WHERE *Camber, East Sussex.*

NOW

Separated from the beautiful beach at Camber by a couple of houses and a huge sand dune is a house described by its owners as a funky surf shack inspired by trips to Montauk, Long Island and Marfa, Texas. Anna Carver, a psychotherapist with a background in advertising, and James Carver, a moving image artist, photographer and co-founder of mindfulness and wellbeing organization NOW.Be present, are serial house flippers. But unlike the traditional flipper, who often seeks maximum profit through minimum effort, the couple collaborate to design homes with soul and authenticity, sourcing reclaimed materials wherever possible and striving to avoid design clichés. When they're done, they are often ready for another challenge so sell up and start all over again.

Lark Rise, as their Camber bungalow is named, is the family's beach house, a place to retreat and kick back. When they purchased the property four years ago it was, as they describe it, a tired and ugly 1980s bungalow. They took down the ceilings and widened the building's footprint on each side, almost completely opening up the space aside from two bedrooms at the front. Along one side of the house are two slender bathrooms and a pantry, a clever use of the narrow strip of floorspace that's been added. Up a spiral staircase and above the bedrooms is a dark, cosy den that's perfect for online gaming.

The interior is the antithesis of the traditional beach house, with rusted corrugated iron walls and black ceilings instead of the predictable whitewashed shiplap, and bold modern art rather than sailboats and seagulls. Such an unexpected interior shouldn't come as a surprise from a pair of self-proclaimed 'disrupters', both of whom have run creative and advertising agencies in the past. Aside from some bathroom sanitaryware and kitchen appliances, very little has been bought brand new. Even the fitted kitchen was personalized with a custom-mixed green paint and Philippe Starck handles that James has taken with him from house to house for 30 years.

Much consideration has gone into the sourcing of materials. The floorboards are reclaimed scaffold boards, while some of the walls were clad in wooden planks salvaged from potato crates. This required a laborious process of dismantling the crates, power-washing the wood and finishing the planks to uniform sizes. Even the doors are clad in lengths of the wood, making them seem to almost disappear into the walls. Other walls are covered in corrugated iron sheets, bought for a pittance from a local farmer who was throwing them away.

Continuing the theme of reclaimed rather than new, most of the furnishings were bought second hand, but because the striking wall finishes dominate the space, furniture has been kept to a minimum – just a sofa, sideboard, dining table, chairs and an eclectic collection of art. Lark Rise is a reminder that when thought and care go into the sourcing and installing of characterful materials, little else is needed.

Beach house reinvented. Knocking through the bungalow's walls and ceilings created a laid-back, open-plan home. The roof was clad in OSB sheets painted matt black. See The Beauty of the Basics section (see pages 20–27) for more ideas on elevating basic building materials. The trusses and steel beams were also painted black and contrast well with the variety of wooden tones and textures.

Farm shop. The majority of the house's walls are clad in materials reclaimed from farms. The wall to the left is clad in wooden strips taken from dismantled potato crates, painstakingly cleaned and cut to uniform sizes before being nailed to the wall in a pleasing arrangement (above and page 84). The bathroom door is also clad with the wooden planks and the same effect was used on the bedroom door (opposite). The other wall is covered with large sheets of rusted corrugated metal (above and page 85). These also wrap around the exterior of the guest room at the end of the garden and were part of a large bundle bought from a local farmer for next to nothing.

But is it art?

A pair of vintage wooden water skis hangs on the reclaimed wooden walls, a nod to nearby sandy shores without veering into the clichéd 'gone fishing' or nautical-themed decor so often seen in beach houses. Mixing different shades of wood can be tricky, but here it works because the silvery tone of the scaffold-board floors and the honey tone of the skis and drum are both repeated in the wall planks.

Where to splurge.

A strong tile or wallpaper can complete and sometimes even inspire a room's design. Here, a patchwork of hand-painted cement tiles by Emery & Cie are a worthy investment, neatly bringing the colour palette together – black ceiling, custom mixed green painted cabinets, concrete worktops, and rust sofa cushions. Adding reclaimed wood to the window jambs is a clever and simple way to customise an often overlooked area.

Use every inch.

A corrugated metal-clad cabin in the garden houses a guest bedroom and bathroom (see pages 94–95). To make better use of the available space, wardrobes/closets were constructed behind a reclaimed wood headboard and wall, providing a simple rail and shelf on each side of the bed. Acquaint yourself with a good carpenter, and bright ideas like this one can become a reality. The painting is by Luke Hannam.

Q&A

5 minutes with Anna & James.

What's the most important thing for you at home?
To make home a place to relax and unwind.

Do you have a decorating/design philosophy?
Our design philosophy is to create inspiring ways to combine authentic materials, space and light. We try to avoid design clichés by mixing up myriad styles of art, surface and furniture.

Do you tend to stay in one property for a long time or do you prefer to move or reinvent your home frequently?
We buy properties that have good potential and then achieve their potential. When we get bored or fancy a change, we move and do it all again.

Describe a creative solution to a challenge you faced with your home
Creating a relaxed environment is key. For example, we chose scaffold-board flooring to encourage people to feel happy to bring sand and mud into the house on their shoes and boots. When it dries, we sweep it up. Simple.

Where do you shop for your home? Do you have a favourite shop/source to recommend?
Anna and I spend a lot of time researching vintage and pre-used items and prefer to buy pre-owned rather than new. We try to find stuff that has a story and character – not bland, boring, predictable or formulaic. Local favourites include Sideshow Interiors in St Leonards and Alex MacArthur Interiors and Soap & Salvation, both in Rye.

Cabin fever. In the guest cabin the reclaimed wood continues, but this time it is contrasted with a shock of custom-mixed yellow paint (opposite). The black ceilings and weathered wooden walls and floors prevent the yellow from feeling overpowering or twee. At one end of the cabin is a bathroom, hidden away behind another wood-clad door (above). To the right is a bench seat and coat hooks, neatly built into a small space by the entrance. The fairground sign came from Sideshow Interiors in St Leonards and adds a dash of tongue-in-cheek humour to the rustic room.

Q&A

5 minutes with Anna & James.

What's the most important thing for you at home?
To make home a place to relax and unwind.

Do you have a decorating/design philosophy?
Our design philosophy is to create inspiring ways to combine authentic materials, space and light. We try to avoid design clichés by mixing up myriad styles of art, surface and furniture.

Do you tend to stay in one property for a long time or do you prefer to move or reinvent your home frequently?
We buy properties that have good potential and then achieve their potential. When we get bored or fancy a change, we move and do it all again.

Describe a creative solution to a challenge you faced with your home.
Creating a relaxed environment is key. For example, we chose scaffold-board flooring to encourage people to feel happy to bring sand and mud into the house on their shoes and boots. When it dries, we sweep it up. Simple.

Where do you shop for your home? Do you have a favourite shop/source to recommend?
Anna and I spend a lot of time researching vintage and pre-used items and prefer to buy pre-owned rather than new. We try to find stuff that has a story and character – not bland, boring, predictable or formulaic. Local favourites include Sideshow Interiors in St Leonards and Alex MacArthur Interiors and Soap & Salvation, both in Rye.

Cabin fever. In the guest cabin the reclaimed wood continues, but this time it is contrasted with a shock of custom-mixed yellow paint (opposite). The black ceilings and weathered wooden walls and floors prevent the yellow from feeling overpowering or twee. At one end of the cabin is a bathroom, hidden away behind another wood-clad door (above). To the right is a bench seat and coat hooks, neatly built into a small space by the entrance. The fairground sign came from Sideshow Interiors in St Leonards and adds a dash of tongue-in-cheek humour to the rustic room.

Sustainable lakeside living.

WHO *Larissa van Seumeren, Peter Kool, Liv Kool (16), Ocean Kool (14) and Bennen Senner Spazey (3).*
WHAT *A climate-neutral self-built lakehouse, 350 sq.m/3767 sq.ft.*
WHERE *Reeuwijk, The Netherlands.*

Sitting on the shore of Reeuwijkse Plassen, one of 13 lakes in Reeuwijk, is this newly built house, one of five developed by project developer and contractor Peter Kool. Peter and his partner, Larissa van Seumeren, designed and built two of the properties, including the one featured here. As well as owning a webstore, The Eye has to Travel, Larissa is an interior designer whose other home was featured in my first book, *Modern Rustic*. It's fascinating to see how a designer's style develops over the years, but even more interesting to see how their core values and signature style remain the same.

Reinventing reclaimed materials and sourcing new items sustainably is at the heart of the couple's designs, just as it was almost ten years ago when we photographed their previous home. This house was designed to be climate neutral, so as well as using lots of recycled materials, they invested in features that would benefit them and the environment. Solar panels provide electricity, plus there's a ground source heat pump for heating and hot water, and triple-glazed windows for optimal insulation.

When I envisage a new build, I can't help but picture white walls and boxy rooms. But Larissa and Peter have created a home with interesting angles and rich textures teamed with a compelling colour palette. The ground floor is mostly open-plan, except for some bedrooms tucked down a hallway. A vaulted ceiling above the kitchen and dining area lets in light from the floor above, and a handmade rope hammock is built into the floor between the two levels. Upstairs there's a chill-out room with views over the lake plus a long hallway with the children's bedrooms ranged along each side. This space has the feel of a cool summer camp like in the movies, only far more stylish.

Throughout the house recycled roof decking was used for many of the walls and floors, with some of the floor planks painted with chalk paint and others left raw. Chalk paint was also used on the walls, ceilings and kitchen cabinets for a seamless look. In the kitchen, the island, which includes the sink, was clad in sheets of copper, with the seams intentionally left rough. Copper also features in the bathrooms, where showers and taps/faucets are fashioned from lengths of copper piping. Just as important as the eco-credentials is the feeling of calm evoked by the colour palette, which manages to be both rich and muted. It was inspired by some handspun and dyed wool that Larissa bought many years before designing the house, and which was later used to create the huge pendant now hanging above the dining table.

It takes dedication and experience to design a home that marries function with form as beautifully as this. Whether it is sourcing materials responsibly, making small changes to lower your home's carbon footprint or finding clever ways to reuse scrap, there is much to be learnt from this Dutch dreamhouse.

Muted palette. In the upstairs chill-out area, reclaimed wooden walls are punctuated with blocks of muted colour (pages 96–97). Off the far corridor are the children's bedrooms, arranged dormitory style. The ground-floor living room is a masterclass in harmonious colour and texture (opposite). The yellow wool rug was designed by the owners and the custom sofa at the rear is covered in recycled denim.

Hand-made touches. Hanging above the dining table is a lampshade that was designed by Larissa and made with yarns whose colours inspired the palette for the house (opposite). The floors are reclaimed brick and add character to the newly built property, while the unpainted steel beam lends an industrial edge. In the kitchen, to the right of the dining area, an island was built with the hob and sink on one side and shelves on the other. These hold a collection of extraordinary handmade tableware that Larissa designed in collaboration with her ceramicist neighbour (above and right). The blue ceramic pendant lights were made in the same way. The island and sink are wrapped in copper sheeting, chosen for its beautiful patination over time (right and above right).

Down to earth. Paint plays a starring role here, with almost every surface covered with Larissa's favourite chalky paint from sustainable eco-friendly brand Pure & Original. Sticking to a cohesive colour palette throughout creates a pleasing sense of flow and won't feel repetitive as long as you vary textures and tones. In one bedroom, mismatched wooden cabinets painted in complementary shades are wall-mounted above a bed (below right). In another, the custom bed has an upholstered headboard that wraps around a corner and is topped with a piece of reclaimed wood to form a shelf (below).

Use every inch.

In the bedroom shown opposite below, a partial wall was added to create space for an ensuite shower room. With proper ventilation, this can be a clever way to break up an interior yet maintain a sense of openness. The taps/faucets (and shower, not shown) were made from copper piping.

Pleasing patina. In the main bedroom, Larissa once again strikes the perfect balance between colour and texture and old and new, also deftly weaving in some family history. The bed was constructed by Peter using beams from an old farmhouse on the land and the asymmetrical headboard is upholstered in a slubby patchwork fabric (opposite above). On the other side of the room, late afternoon light floods the bathroom, where a free-standing tub holds centre stage. The bath was Larissa's grandparents and her own father bathed in it as a child (above).

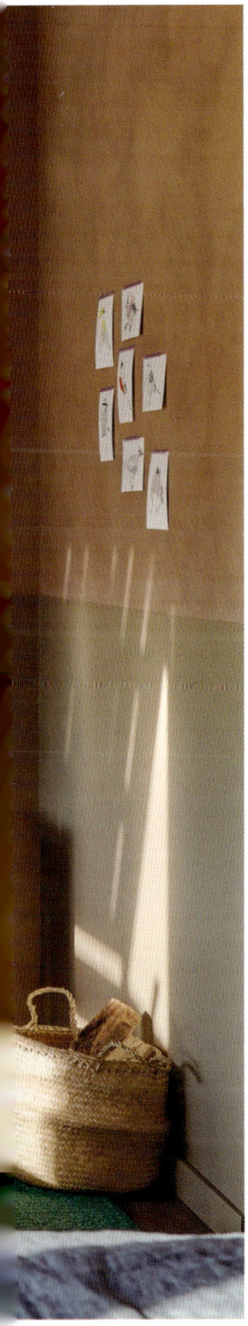

Q&A

5 minutes with Larissa & Peter.

What's the most important thing for you at home?
This house was designed and built as a family home. Our whole family – my parents, my brother and his three children (and dog) and our own family – use the house during holidays and on weekends. Besides this, it's used by close friends and relatives. The values at the heart of the design were optimal views of the lake and its surroundings. A light, airy feeling and at the same time a warm, cosy, and laid-back atmosphere. Space to relax and unwind alone or in a small group. And the opportunity to be outside as much as possible.

Do you have a decorating/design philosophy?
Think about how you live and translate that into a personalized design that suits you. Take your time – a house must grow on you and with you – and only collect or purchase what really makes your heart beat faster. In that case, it will last a lifetime.

Describe a creative solution to a challenge you faced with your home.
We wanted a climate-neutral house with lots of recycled and natural materials. Peter made the bed in the master bedroom from the beams of an old farmhouse and the bathtub is from my grandparents' house – my father was washed in it when he was a little child! In addition to being better for the environment, it also gives the house more character.

Where do you shop for your home? Do you have a favourite store or source?
My own store, The Eye Has To Travel (theeyehastotravel.nl), of course! Also Anthropologie, Studio de Winkel (Dutch design from small designers) Catawiki and Marktplaats (art, vintage and antique items). Couleur Locale (African crafts), Homestock (a Dutch chain offering colourful home accessories), IKEA, Sissy-Boy (homewares), Urban Outfitters, Les Petits Bohemes and By Mölle (both beautiful textiles), Return to Sender (Dutch design plus handcrafts from developing countries) and Etsy.

Do you prefer to stay in one property for a long time or do you like to move or reinvent your home frequently?
Personally, I like to go places. I lived in Utrecht for 10 years and now we're in a rural area with our growing kids as we want to give them a good foundation. But in the future, we dream of renting out our home and going around the world in a campervan.

WHO *Manonne Kemper-Boerema and Remco Kemper, children Nola Elvis (18), Nikki Lois (16) and Tommy Sidh (12) and cats Puck and Pien.*
WHAT *A former bleachery, with parts dating back to the 17th century, 420 sq.m/ 4520 sq.ft.*
WHERE *Heemstede, The Netherlands.*

A Dutch cabinet of curiosities.

Manonne and Remco have been renovating their house since 2008. To some, this might sound like a nightmare, but I understand completely. There is much to be said for renovating and decorating over time. Aside from the obvious point of not having to pour bucketloads of money into a home all at one time, it also allows ideas to percolate and evolve.

Before moving in, the couple spent six months completing essential structural works (roof, flooring, plumbing) alongside a contractor. Due to many years of neglect, there was an enormous amount of work to do. Luckily Remco is very capable and has carried out much of the work himself over the years. When the family moved in, there was not a functioning bathroom or kitchen so their two eldest children, toddlers at the time, took baths in a plastic tub in the 'kitchen'. The upstairs wasn't even used for the first six years, but because the property is so big it was easy to live around the ongoing updates.

Manonne is a former hair and make-up artist and Remco works as a freelance product development and business consultant. He also works occasionally as an interior architect, a factor that has been beneficial in the development of the property. They also have a small business developing accessories for wheelchair users (quokkabag.com). In addition, Manonne is starting a new business renting out decorative tableware and flower arches. How they manage to keep all these plates spinning as well as raise a family and renovate a house is anyone's guess, but somehow they do.

The property sits parallel to a small canal, which was dug centuries ago to allow ships to deliver linen to these buildings for bleaching and treating. The oldest part dates to the late 17th century, but the main house was built in 1880 with additions made in 1921. The property is wider than it is tall, much of it occupying the sprawling ground floor with bedrooms and bathrooms above. It is a stylish hodgepodge of materials; a patchwork of exposed bricks, metal beams, woodwork, concrete floors and reclaimed elements. In 2017 the couple purchased the neighbouring building, its ground floor becoming a cavernous room with an impressive full-height brick wall while the upper floor was converted into an apartment for Remco's father.

The home is furnished entirely with vintage and reclaimed pieces, except for the kitchen appliances and stainless steel work surfaces. The kitchen walls are bare plasterboard, waiting for the time when the couple have saved enough for the vintage tiles they've set their hearts on. Many of the walls retain exposed building materials or the original paint colours, adding to a sense of authenticity. Slow, thoughtful decorating is the name of the game here, and it's a wonderful reminder to accept that a home is a work in progress – and that is OK.

Salvage style. Except for the odd kitchen appliance, I challenge you to find anything new in this cabinet of curiosities. The metal staircase (page 106) was salvaged from a building where it was an external feature and Remco adapted it to fit their stairs. The living-room sofa was built from pallets while the pot rack in the kitchen was once a train luggage rack (page 107 and opposite). Concrete floors throughout offer a solid and contemporary base for the eclectic furnishings and raw finishes of this expansive home.

Work in progress.

The kitchen wall is prepped and ready for the vintage tiles the couple plan to buy when they are ready to spend. Rather than settle for something they don't love in order to finish the job, they live – for now – with bare plasterboard. They've prioritized practicality, making sure the kitchen functions but leaving the door open for the final touch.

Industrial chic. The kitchen units have been pieced together using a commercial stainless steel sink/work surface fixed atop a simple wooden structure (opposite). Linen curtains conceal open shelves that hold all the kitchen stuff we need but don't want on display. The utilitarian stainless steel countertop and range cooker work well against the rougher finishes of the reclaimed pieces, from the utensil jars to the dining table (right and above right). Above the table hang two huge reclaimed factory lights, adding a sense of industrial drama to the otherwise demure country-style room (above). This part of the building was added in 1921 and the iron windows are original. Just visible in the back garden is a pile of reclaimed bricks, poised for use in yet another project, the patio.

Lateral flow. When the property next door came up for sale the couple bought it, adding a separate apartment upstairs for Remco's father. They completed as much of the renovations as possible before knocking through a wall to connect the two properties (above). The new space is one huge room with double doors leading to the home office, from which Manonne and Remco run their businesses. The ceiling height is immense and feels dramatic, especially since the chimney breast is also full height (opposite). The rear façade was retained, with new (old) brick extending up from it and connecting it to the vaulted wooden ceiling (above right). Because of the room's scale, everything is supersized, from lighting to artwork to houseplants (right).

COTE DOR

All serene. The majority of the home's footprint is on the ground floor and upstairs there are just the bedrooms. The main bedroom is a serene oasis in calming shades of white, and because the room is tucked under the eaves it boasts lovely light from the skylights (above and above right). The couple are fortunate to have a large built-in wardrobe/closet (not pictured), adding to the sense of calm order. Additional storage is concealed behind a small door to the side of the bed.

Q&A

5 minutes with Manonne & Remco.

Do you have a decorating/design philosophy?
Even though we have (structurally) renovated the largest part of the house, our aim has always been to make it look as if the place has been like this forever. We like the house to have a relaxed atmosphere, and although we have a lot of old pieces, it should not be a museum. We also like to reuse old materials and furniture. Our taste is not very modern, even though design classics like the LC4 [chaise longue] and our Gispen chairs are close to our heart. The effect is somewhat eclectic, because of all the plants that Manonne finds and the accessories Remco brings from his travels.

Where do you shop for your home? Do you have a favourite store or source?
Our local eBay (Marktplaats.nl) has been the biggest source, both for building materials and furniture and accessories. We like materials and furniture with a history. Our old neighbour used to call our house the 'Wunderkammer', as it is full of curiosities and old stuff. Since the house is so big, we have been forced to spend our money in a smart way. Our contractor says; 'Big houses, big bills', but he also tries to keep costs low by recycling materials and coming up with creative solutions. Next to Marktplaats, the internet in general is a big help in finding specific items. The key is to be patient and persistent. For some of the antique building materials we go to a fantastic dealer close to the Belgium border (Benko.nl) that sells exceptional stuff. Remco's father used to be an antiques dealer and he provided us with the three old chimneypieces we have in the house.

Do you prefer to stay in one property for a long time or do you like to move or reinvent your home frequently?
Well, as you may have gathered by now, our house is an ongoing project so there is actually no need to move!

Is there any other work you're planning to do?
Our last big project has been the garden, which is now in the last stages of completion. However, inside we still have a lot to do.

Simple chic. Square white tiles – firmly back in fashion – are the epitome of function combined with simple beauty (avoid white grout for easier cleaning). A pair of vintage sinks and industrial wall lights scream retro hospital style, but this bathroom feels chic not cold (above).

Rashid Johnson
REBECCA HORN
THIS IS HOME

The brewery barn.

WHO *Misty Buckley, Reggie Matheson, their children Indiana (10) and Dusty-Rose (9) and cats Biffy and Berry.*
WHAT *The Barn, part of an old brewery, 164 sq.m/1765 sq.ft.*
WHERE *Pilton, Somerset.*

In 2018 Misty Buckley and Reggie Matheson had been living at the Storehouse for a few years (see pages 72–83), part of an old brewery in the Somerset village close to where the Glastonbury Festival takes place. They were thoughtfully renovating it, filling it with reclaimed furniture, flooring and lighting and slowly making a home for their family of four, when they discovered that the adjoining building was for sale. The vast barn had been owned separately for 80 years, most recently by a sculptor who, along with her son, taught sculpture and life-drawing classes. The sellers wanted the barn to remain a creative space, and Misty and Reggie, thrilled to reunite the two buildings, were more than happy to oblige.

For a couple of years the building remained unchanged, with holes in the roof and pencil markings of students' names and kiln timings scribbled on the wall. When the Covid-19 pandemic hit and home schooling became the norm, the family were grateful to have the space to spread out. During the second UK lockdown, the old tiled roof was replaced, insulation was added and the crumbling walls were rendered with modern lime plaster, with care taken to retain the original contours and character. When the plaster set, the couple fell in love with its creamy colour and texture and decided to leave it unpainted. The concrete floor, with evidence of its past life as an artist's studio to be seen here and there, was also left untouched, as were the original beams and large cathedral windows.

In keeping with the couple's decorating ethos, the palette is a natural one and their commitment to using pieces with a history continues. Due to the vast scale of the barn, it is zoned into areas – cooking and lounging at one end, dining and crafting at the long table in the middle, and more creating and working at the other end. But you get the sense that everything here is flexible, with many of the furnishings set on casters for easy mobility.

When the barn was rewired, the couple added lights and switches sourced from an old factory in eastern Europe, with the electrical conduits deliberately left on display. The 'slow kitchen', as Misty and Reggie named it, revealed itself over time as they gradually sourced the elements that would eventually make it whole. Stainless steel appliances contrast with a large butler's sink perched on a stand of painted brick, the plywood worktops are a temporary stand-in for the reclaimed marble they hope to find some day, and the reclaimed draper's table was sourced from a bookshop that was closing down. Even the extractor fan is disguised by a raw plastered frame, with plants arranged on top. It seems that with a clear vision, a willing team of builders and a deliberately slow pace, Misty and Reggie have managed to create somewhere that feels both nurturing and inviting, a space to be lived in and from which to create.

Fabric softener. At the living-room end of the large barn, layers of sheepskins and other textiles bring a cohesive feel to an eclectic grouping of furniture (pages 116–117 and opposite). The old sofa is draped in a slubby linen dropcloth and piled with cushions, and a coffee table has been fashioned from an old trunk that was given a lick of teal paint and also doubles up as storage.

Clever zoning.

Large pieces of furniture can be used to create defined zones within an open-plan space. Misty and Reggie fixed this old draper's counter onto casters for easy mobility. When in this position the kitchen area is larger, but the counter can also be turned parallel to the wall to open the space up more.

Movable feast. Because it's intended to be a flexible space, almost everything in the barn is on casters and can be moved around to accommodate a particular activity or event. Because of the ceiling height, large strings of festoon lights, usually seen outdoors, work really well, drawing the eye up and, of course, adding a magical glow in the evenings when the wood burner is fired up and drinks are flowing. Large reclaimed factory shelving units (on casters, of course) are endlessly useful, and adding smaller bins/boxes keeps the shelves organized (opposite).

Q&A

5 minutes with Misty & Reggie.

What's the most important thing for you at home?
The barn is flexible and I am not at all precious about it. If plates get dropped or something breaks, it adds to the charm of the place – except the amazing olive oil pots from Kiln Home. Those are unique pieces!

Do you have a decorating/design philosophy?
Like the Storehouse, the colour palette is restrained, but we went a little softer in here. When the plaster first dried to a beautiful creamy colour with loads of natural depth and variation, we made the decision not to paint it. It's warm and earthy and we have continued that throughout the space. When you walk in, it has this incredibly serene energy. I find it a calming space to work, cook, read or make.

Describe a creative solution to a challenge you faced with your home?
I think the success story in the barn is the lighting and the electrical fittings. Paul is an incredible electrician who totally gets my aesthetic, along with our builder Edd. We're lucky in Somerset – we have some craftspeople who really care and take their time.

Where do you shop for your home? Do you have a favourite store or source?
This space is large and anything too small looks a bit weedy in here. We found the draper's counter online when a bookseller in Hay-on-Wye was closing down. The huge art cupboard was a great find in a reclamation yard – somebody had just returned it because they couldn't fit it in their house. It was still on the back of the truck and we spotted it, made an offer and the truck continued straight on to our place!

Do you prefer to stay in one property for a long time or do you like to move or reinvent your home frequently?
I always look for a new project, but this one is fulfilling for the moment. There are incredible cellars downstairs that would make a beautiful apartment – I have tear sheets of Tuscan vaulted farmhouses! Oh, and an old stable block outside. So I'm good for the minute!

Is there any other work you're planning to do?
I would love to get a kiln and a potter's wheel back in here. There used to be an enormous kiln here and I love that you can still see the plaster marks on the floor.

Practical and handsome. In the kitchen area, a chunky butler's sink rests on painted brick pillars (above). An old metal trunk sitting on a plywood dolly fits perfectly into the cavity below and is a stylish way to conceal cleaning supplies. The temporary kitchen worksurface is plywood, an inexpensive placeholder for the reclaimed marble counters that Misty and Reggie hope to fit one day. Meanwhile, a slab of marble serves as a chopping block and hints at what's to come (above left). Throughout the barn, the electrical conduits were surface mounted, a design decision that saved on the cost of chasing electrical wiring into the walls (left). Two long trestle tables sit side by side to create a large work surface and white paint unifies them with mismatched wooden chairs (opposite).

A post office reinvented.

WHO *Karone Pack-Lum and Jon Agrippa.*
WHAT *A post office and sorting depot dating from 1910, 176 sq.m/1895 sq.ft.*
WHERE *Kent coast.*

Buying three floors of a 1910 post office and sorting depot in need of redevelopment was not what Karone Pack-Lum and Jon Agrippa had in mind when they decided to leave London and move to the Kent coast. They originally had their sights set on a big old brick house, but the sale fell through. When they heard about this property through word of mouth – it wasn't even listed – they immediately recognized an exciting opportunity: good bones, a unique building, a great location and a creative challenge.

Self-described die-hard Londoners, the couple previously lived in East London, Jon working in fashion and Karone in interiors. But they were tiring of city life and craved a more peaceful lifestyle that didn't revolve around paying the mortgage. Their seaside life is a far cry from their fast-paced London days. Jon is now a personal trainer and Karone designs jewellery while taking on the occasional interior design project.

Once they'd found the property in this up-and-coming coastal town, they struggled to find builders who could carry out work within their budget. The section of the sorting depot they bought hadn't been developed like the rest of the building – in fact it was nothing but a shell. There were no electrics, gas supply or even stairs connecting the three floors. The lower level – now the main living area – had been a loading bay and had two huge openings in the walls, as big as the Crittall-style windows that now fill that space. The upper floor, where the main bedroom now sits, was a warren of staff rooms and toilets, with a gaping hole in the floor where a shute dropped down to basement level.

At first sight the home looks luxe, and certainly money has been spent here. But much of the budget went into the structural changes necessary to convert the building from a mail sorting depot into a home. The couple moved in once the major structural changes were complete, but the decorative work is an ongoing process. Karone and Jon sought cost-effective ways of achieving the look they desired and worked with existing finishes and flooring wherever possible. Many of the walls are finished with bare plaster, a look they love and which has the added bonus of saving on a hefty painting bill. The kitchen was built from moisture-resistant MDF and left unpainted, which was intended as a temporary cost-effective solution to tide them over until they build their 'real' kitchen. However, they have grown to love it and may simply update it with a green marble worksurface in the future.

Most of the lighting and furnishings are second hand, bought at house clearances, on eBay or from salvage yards. Even the luxurious bathtub was found on eBay and many other items that look like pricey designer pieces were discovered through diligent searching. Karone claims that it is possible to get deals on almost everything if you're willing to look around: 'It is truly amazing the amount of stuff that is ripped out and thrown away.'

Luxe looks. In a prime example of basic building materials looking luxe, the walls throughout are finished in hard-wearing gypsum plaster, their soft textured grey finish bouncing light around the lower level of the home (pages 124 and 125). The ceilings remain as found and the stairs were added to connect the ground floor to the lower level. Light from the entrance hallway seeps through a cut-out at the top of the stairs.

When to splurge.

This area was once a loading bay and had two van-sized holes in the wall. One was filled in while the other was fitted with custom-made windows. Savings were made elsewhere – an old sofa was draped in linen instead of being replaced and the lighting is second hand.

Soothing spaces. Upstairs in the guest bedroom, things are simple and calming, with natural linen bedding and a sisal rug (left). The original window frames were painted black and contrast well with the plastered walls. In the main bathroom, a contractor was hired to apply dark grey micro-cement to all surfaces (above right and opposite). The bath was found second hand on eBay and the vanity was designed by Karone, who topped a painted wooden cabinet with a concrete sink. In the guest bathroom, Jon decided to bypass the professionals and try his hand at micro-cementing the space himself, this time in a lighter tone (above left). With the help of online tutorials, he succeeded in cocooning the wet room in an earthy oatmeal colour that is soft and smooth to the touch.

When to splurge.

This area was once a loading bay and had two van-sized holes in the wall. One was filled in while the other was fitted with custom-made windows. Savings were made elsewhere – an old sofa was draped in linen instead of being replaced and the lighting is second hand.

Let there be light. The kitchen was built from green water-resistant MDF as a cheap temporary solution and the floors are screed. The high windows are at street level, which demonstrates the necessity for new windows to flood the space with light. Artwork is minimal and the colour palette is muted, with elements from nature adding a hint of green.

Soothing spaces. Upstairs in the guest bedroom, things are simple and calming, with natural linen bedding and a sisal rug (left). The original window frames were painted black and contrast well with the plastered walls. In the main bathroom, a contractor was hired to apply dark grey micro-cement to all surfaces (above right and opposite). The bath was found second hand on eBay and the vanity was designed by Karone, who topped a painted wooden cabinet with a concrete sink. In the guest bathroom, Jon decided to bypass the professionals and try his hand at micro-cementing the space himself, this time in a lighter tone (above left). With the help of online tutorials, he succeeded in cocooning the wet room in an earthy oatmeal colour that is soft and smooth to the touch.

5826
5820
LIVE BEAUTIFUL

Original features. In the guest bedroom (opposite right), the original tile was painted with a black band and vintage coat hooks/hangers were added. In the main bedroom (this page), once the post office staff room, bright green paint was scrubbed off to reveal the original tile. The parquet is also original. In the hallway, old radiators were painted black and copper pipes were left unpainted.

Q&A

5 minutes with Karone & Jon.

Do you have a decorating/design philosophy?
We like to work with the space using a limited colour palette, then adding texture.

What's the most important thing for you at home?
Loving where you live is key.

Where do you shop for your home?
I like scouring online auctions e.g. eBay, Facebook Marketplace and also salvage and house clearance.

Describe one of your favourite creative solutions to a challenge you faced with your home?
The whole build was a creative solution. We had many people such as the architect, builders and numerous others convinced that we could not achieve our goal on the budget we had – hey, what did they know!

Do you prefer to stay in one property for a long time or do you like moving or even re-inventing your home frequently?
We tend to stay put.

Is there something you haven't done to your home yet and would like to?
There is definitely a list of both cosmetic and essential jobs that we are working our way through.

Handmade in Bristol.

WHO *Francesca Gaskin.*
WHAT *A two-bedroom Victorian terraced/row house, 74 sq.m/796 sq.ft.*
WHERE *St Werburghs, Bristol.*

Born and raised in London, designer Francesca Gaskin knew that getting on the housing ladder in that notoriously expensive city was increasingly unlikely, particularly on a freelance salary. In 2018, she and a group of friends decided to move to Bristol, a city brimming with creativity and culture.

After renting for a year while viewing countless properties, Francesca bought a two-bedroom Victorian terraced/row house. Little did she know that this would lead to the launch of her own business, Jetsam Made, which specializes in bespoke kitchens and furniture.

Her new home's decor hadn't been updated in decades, but it was solid in terms of structure – roof, windows and so on. And luckily it didn't have a new kitchen or bathroom, so Francesca didn't have to feel guilty about ripping those out because she wanted to design her own. She lived in the house for six months, getting a feel for the light and space while obtaining quotes from contractors to see what she could afford. However, not long after this, the Covid-19 pandemic hit and she was made redundant. Her small budget now had to stretch even further, but at least the extra time enabled her to save money in some areas by teaching herself to do a lot of the work on her own.

With a degree in interior architecture and a couple of years freelancing in set building for film, floristry and production under her belt, Francesca is clearly a woman who can set her hand at pretty much anything. But it was her job in a Bristol workshop where she learned joinery and steel fabrication that equipped her with the skills to design and hand-build her entire kitchen from powder-coated steel and birch ply during the Covid lockdowns/stay-at-home orders.

We may not all be able to build our own kitchen units, but in her home Francesca has employed a number of more accessible creative solutions. Colour plays an important role here, with simple paint effects packing a punch in most rooms. Doors, cornices/crown moldings and skirtings/baseboards are painted in varying and sometimes contrasting shades, an easy way to add colour and interest. In the kitchen a border of pale blue is painted at the top of the bare plaster walls, giving the illusion of a cornice/crown molding. The notion of leaving plastered walls bare, the chalky pink finish sealed only with decorator's varnish, is becoming increasingly popular and works well in both period and more contemporary homes.

Throughout her home, Francesca has introduced furniture and accessories sourced on eBay or in vintage shops, as well as hand-me-downs from family. It is the contrast between the cool modernity of her kitchen and the eclectic mix in the other rooms that makes this such an interesting interior. It is a home that expresses all the different sides of the owner's style and refuses to fit into a prescribed box.

Plaster and ply. In the kitchen/diner, Francesca left the freshly plastered walls bare, sealing them and adding a stripe of blue paint where the wall meets the ceiling (opposite). She built the birch plywood and steel kitchen cabinets herself, as well as the table (pages 134 and 135). The bench seating doubles as storage and was built from glass blocks sourced on eBay. There are LED lights inside the cubes, with colours changeable by remote control.

Colour therapy. In the snug living room at the front of the house, a bold vintage sofa is draped with a throw to hide signs of wear and the eclectic mix of textiles is calmed by the colour block mustard curtains and cushions (this page and opposite). The wooden floors and the walls have been painted but the ceilings are raw plaster and a darker shade of mustard coats the cornice/crown molding, creating drama in an often overlooked area.

Q&A

5 minutes with Francesca.

What's the most important thing for you at home?
The most important thing is creativity and being in a space that inspires and is beautiful to me, surrounded by all my possessions that remind me of people that I love and experiences I have had.

Do you have a decorating/design philosophy?
I try not to follow trends, I go with things that I like, and from this a personal style will develop. I often have a starting point. In the instance of my kitchen, it was a photograph that I took at the Burning Man festival of a dusty pink shipping container in the desert. I wanted the kitchen to represent this image, which was done through choices of colours and textures. Ultimately, I think that investing in good design and choosing things that make you happy and that you like to look at will stand the test of time.

Describe a creative solution to a challenge you faced with your home.
It would have to be the kitchen. There were a couple of reasons for designing it myself: I didn't want a standard-looking kitchen and had a vision in my mind of what I wanted. It was also to save money. Also adding the large picture window in the kitchen. This off-the-shelf window has changed the room dramatically, making what was once a dark space into a light, airy one.

Where do you shop for your home? Do you have a favourite store or source?
I have mostly collected items from family members. I love eBay for vintage furniture, random finds or building materials, such as vintage glass bricks or the Chinese fabric I used to make drapes for my bed. And I love Retrouvius. The 1920s vintage rug in the sitting room from Retrouvius was a gift to myself when I bought the house (and is actually the most expensive thing in the house).

Do you prefer to stay in one property for a long time or do you like to move or reinvent your home frequently?
This is the first home that I have made my mark on and I am totally in love with it and grateful to own it. But further down the line I would love to buy some land and build a house from scratch.

Is there any other work you're planning to do?
I studied for my Royal Horticultural Society Level 2 qualification in horticulture during the pandemic so I'm dying to finish the garden. I've built raised beds myself, learning bricklaying and rendering from YouTube. The patio has been sourced from eBay and most of the plants were saved from skips/dumpsters or given to me by friends and family. I would also love to convert the loft but again it's down to budget, so it will have to wait.

Creative solutions. The bathroom budget was tight, but Francesca had time on her hands during lockdowns so decided to tackle the task herself. She tiled the wall around the bath as well as plumbing in all the bathroom fixtures. There were a few disasters along the way, but nothing she couldn't sort out by referring to YouTube videos. She found the baby blue sink on the street the week she was scheduled to tackle the plumbing and updated it with contemporary black taps/ faucets. The sink and toilet are different colours and styles, something that can add character. The walls are a creation of her own design, the finish achieved by layering different shades of a special textured spray paint, available in many DIY shops.

But is it art?

Using fabric she sourced on eBay, Francesca created two identical panels that she hung from her four-poster bed. She lined them with wadding/batting so the finished panels have a nice weight and hang well from their fabric tabs. It's a clever way to make use of the bedposts to create a headboard/textile art hybrid.

CARLO PONTI
MICHELANGELO ANTONIONI
BLOW-UP
LION
JUST KIDS
PATTI SMITH

A retro-modern new-build.

WHO *Emma Jane Palin and Joshua John Parker plus George, their Chiweenie dog.*
WHAT *A three-bedroom townhouse built in 2021, 95 sq.m/1022 sq.ft.*
WHERE *Ramsgate, Kent.*

When planning this book, I hoped to include Emma Jane Palin's Margate flat as an excellent example of a creative and inexpensive update of a rented home. However, by the time photography began, interior stylist and blogger Emma and her husband Joshua, a musician, had bought a house in nearby Ramsgate. I hesitated about including their new home as my focus here is on creativity rather than consumption and it would be misleading to say that new things hadn't been bought for this home. But when I heard it was a new build, I was intrigued. As more affordable housing is built to meet demand for a growing population – and particularly for first-time buyers wanting to take advantage of the UK government's 'Help to Buy' scheme, as Emma and Joshua did – a lot of characterless new builds are going to need some decorating inspiration. The couple have done a great job of adding character with creative and conscious consumption, mixing vintage pieces with independent designers and makers as well as a bit of high street – still necessary for many people on a tight budget.

As new builds go, this one is well-planned with an attractive exterior and good interior flow. Tucked away on a small street near the centre of town and the harbour, the townhouses are reminiscent of stylish warehouses, with brick and wood facades, black-framed windows and small back gardens that sit alongside the larger communal garden of a neighbouring building. The couple hadn't considered buying a new build before, but this one kept popping up in their property searches and when their mortgage broker said it was affordable, they went for it. And as they are the first owners of the home, they didn't have to spend money on any refurbishments or improvements, which freed up more of the budget for decorating.

As fans of fashion and interiors from the 1960s and 70s, the couple set about layering colours, patterns and furnishings inspired by these decades. The walls are painted in shades of white and palest pink, allowing colourful furnishings and artwork to stand out. The furniture is a mix of vintage, such as the orange bucket sofa found on a secondhand online marketplace, designer pieces bought on sale and high-street finds. A few pieces were designed by Emma in collaboration with sustainable homeware brand Kalinko. But it's in the office/music den that the couple's 70s dreams are made manifest, with dark ceilings, chain-link wallpaper and a floor-to-ceiling cork wall, serving as an ever-evolving moodboard.

With plans to update the kitchen and bathrooms, it will be exciting to see how the space evolves. Homes develop over time, but I tip my hat to Emma and Joshua for adding so much style and character to a blank slate in such a short amount of time.

Retro spirit. In the dining nook to the side of the living room, a vintage chrome and smoked glass table found on eBay is circled by dining chairs from West Elm and lit by a pendant from Tom Dixon. On the wall, album covers are displayed in meticulously lined-up rows – a simple but effective way to create a gallery wall with treasures from the music-loving couple's vinyl collection. The orange velour modular sofa and mirrored side table (pages 142–143) were found for a steal on eBay.

pish
Françoise Hardy
Black Honey
THE ROLLING STONES
NICO CHELSEA GIRL
LET IT BE
NICK CAVE AND THE BAD SEEDS

Careful consumption. Although many pieces in their home were bought new, Emma and Joshua have tried to buy the best that they can afford with the intention of keeping new possessions for a long time. It's not always possible to buy everything second hand, but if you can invest in pieces for the long term and choose materials that don't hurt the environment too much, that also helps. In the main bedroom (above and above right) the bed and bedside tables/nightstands are from Urban Outfitters and the sideboard is from Tylko. The cushions on the bed include one designed by Emma in collaboration with sustainable homewares brand Kalinko and the painting above the bed is by Studio Lenca. In the guest bedroom (right) the bed is by Sebastian Cox for Made.com, and the green shaded lamp is Luke Edward Hall x Habitat.

But is it art?

Wardrobe/closet doors were removed and the interior was customized with paper and paint from Lust Home, creating a display cabinet for Emma's clothing. This works best if your clothes are pleasing to look at and you are tidy, but even a dress hung on a hook can become a work of art.

Retro dreams. In their home office/music room, Emma and Joshua are living out their mid-century dreams with a chainlink wallpaper by Poodle and Blonde. On one wall, they applied self-adhesive cork tiles to create an evolving moodboard for daily inspiration (opposite). Cork is highly sustainable and also makes an excellent floor covering.

Q&A

5 minutes with Emma & Joshua.

What's the most important thing for you at home?
To express our personalities and surround us with things we love. Music, art and fashion are important to both of us, and I think that's evident as soon as you step in the door.

Do you have a decorating/design philosophy?
I see so much interiors inspiration on a daily basis and while I appreciate different styles and trends, I try to stay true to my own style. I hate the thought of not liking a room in a short period of time. It's important to note that without a ton of money, things are going to take time and you are free to experiment with your personal style. Everyone makes mistakes when decorating and you'll develop your style over the years.

Describe a creative solution to a challenge you faced with your home?
We've yet to tackle anything too expensive with the house but I always look to do things myself to avoid labour costs, plus I like learning. I paid for an upholstery course, which feels a better use of money as I will learn something new. In the bedroom we've built a huge window seat and I'm cladding this with bamboo as well as upholstering a 3.5 m/11ft cushion for it. The cork walls in the office are also an inexpensive way of adding texture to a space without any structural work and you can change the look of them frequently.

Where do you shop for your home? Do you have a favourite store or source?
I like a mixture of secondhand and new with a focus on high-end design. We found our vintage 1970s modular sofa on eBay for £300 and I also love to browse Facebook Marketplace and Narchie for secondhand buys. My favourite independent shop for decor is W.A.Green, but I also look at John Lewis and Dunelm for high-street buys.

Do you like to stay in one property for a long time or do you prefer moving or reinventing your home frequently?
As we rented for such a long time and moved quite frequently (we've lived in five homes in our seven years together), this space is going to be a slow work in progress. I like to decorate in a timeless way as I find the upheaval quite stressful.

What's next for your home?
The next thing on my list is the kitchen. We'll use the existing cabinetry and give it a makeover with paint. I've seen a hack to strip laminate cupboards using a hairdryer! I'd love to create a luxurious-feeling kitchen on a budget, so watch this space.

Use every inch.

Ruth's rail of multicoloured garments screens the bedroom area. On the living-room side sits a desk that doubles as work space by day and sewing table by night. Sourced from a dealer in the Netherlands, the couple later discovered the vintage piece was originally from a rattan specialist in Germany.

Use every inch.

Ruth's rail of multicoloured garments screens the bedroom area. On the living-room side sits a desk that doubles as work space by day and sewing table by night. Sourced from a dealer in the Netherlands, the couple later discoverd the vintage piece was originally from a rattan specialist in Germany.

Clever zoning.

Despite the completely open-plan layout of the loft, Ruth and Cory created a private bedroom area, tucked away discreetly at the back of the room behind a clothing rail and a drinks cabinet. The two large pillars help to demarcate the three distinct areas – sleeping, living and eating. As shown here, rugs can be useful for defining an area, even if your space is smaller than this one.

Q&A

5 minutes with Emma & Joshua.

What's the most important thing for you at home?
To express our personalities and surround us with things we love. Music, art and fashion are important to both of us, and I think that's evident as soon as you step in the door.

Do you have a decorating/design philosophy?
I see so much interiors inspiration on a daily basis and while I appreciate different styles and trends, I try to stay true to my own style. I hate the thought of not liking a room in a short period of time. It's important to note that without a ton of money, things are going to take time and you are free to experiment with your personal style. Everyone makes mistakes when decorating and you'll develop your style over the years.

Describe a creative solution to a challenge you faced with your home?
We've yet to tackle anything too expensive with the house but I always look to do things myself to avoid labour costs, plus I like learning. I paid for an upholstery course, which feels a better use of money as I will learn something new. In the bedroom we've built a huge window seat and I'm cladding this with bamboo as well as upholstering a 3.5 m/11ft cushion for it. The cork walls in the office are also an inexpensive way of adding texture to a space without any structural work and you can change the look of them frequently.

Where do you shop for your home? Do you have a favourite store or source?
I like a mixture of secondhand and new with a focus on high-end design. We found our vintage 1970s modular sofa on eBay for £300 and I also love to browse Facebook Marketplace and Narchie for secondhand buys. My favourite independent shop for decor is W.A.Green, but I also look at John Lewis and Dunelm for high-street buys.

Do you like to stay in one property for a long time or do you prefer moving or reinventing your home frequently?
As we rented for such a long time and moved quite frequently (we've lived in five homes in our seven years together), this space is going to be a slow work in progress. I like to decorate in a timeless way as I find the upheaval quite stressful.

What's next for your home?
The next thing on my list is the kitchen. We'll use the existing cabinetry and give it a makeover with paint. I've seen a hack to strip laminate cupboards using a hairdryer! I'd love to create a luxurious-feeling kitchen on a budget, so watch this space.

Loft life in East Berlin.

WHO *Ruth Bartlett, Cory Andreen and their two long-haired chihuahuas, Daddy and Enya.*
WHAT *An open-plan loft in an old factory building, 85 sq.m/ 914 sq.ft.*
WHERE *Kreuzberg, Berlin.*

Hidden behind two sets of huge graffitied doors, across a courtyard lined with bicycles and flower-filled bathtubs, and at the top of quite a few flights of stairs, sits this loft apartment. Located in Kreuzberg, a vibrant, multicultural district of Berlin bustling with cafes, galleries, and food markets, the loft is home to Ruth Bartlett and husband Cory Andreen. Ruth is a set designer and originally from the UK, while Cory, an American, owns beverage company Motel, producing specialist coffee and beer. Sharing the space (and adding some canine style with their pearl dog collars) are the couple's long-haired chihuahuas Daddy and Enya.

Unlike other parts of the world where home ownership is the goal, many Berliners happily rent long-term with no plan to buy property. Because of this, renters are often free to make changes usually reserved for owners. It isn't unusual to move into a rented apartment that has no kitchen because the previous tenants installed their own and took it with them when they left. Cory has rented this loft since 2013, with Ruth moving in around 2018, and together they've managed to put their stamp on the space without any major structural works, instead using an eclectic blend of old, new and sentimental finds. In terms of DIY, together they have most bases covered, with Ruth's set design skills equipping her for woodwork and textile projects and Cory able to tackle anything involving electrics and water.

Through clever spatial planning the couple have created distinct areas within the loft, but aside from a small bathroom and a tiny hallway it is completely open-plan. Not all couples could cohabitat in this way, but Ruth and Cory say that it works well for them. Working with the existing structure of the space, they have divided it into three main areas: cooking and eating, living and entertaining, and sleeping and dressing. Clothing rails and a drinks cabinet conceal the 'bedroom' area at the back of the loft while a vintage rug delineates the 'living room'. The 5-m/16-ft ceilings, south-facing windows and skylights add a luxurious amount of daylight that makes the space feel bright and airy despite the maximal decor.

I loved Ruth's reference to Marie Kondo, usually known for her minimalist interiors, and her instruction to keep only what sparks joy (see page 158). For Ruth, this is true of every piece they own, and it's the joyful and creative mix of styles, eras, patterns and colours that makes this home so intriguing. Every piece tells a story, whether it's the heavy marble coffee table, found on eBay and lugged up many flights of stairs, or the patchwork quilt on the sofa that was handmade by Ruth, or the pizza boxes hung on their gallery wall, designed in collaboration by a local tattoo parlour and pizza maker. For this creative couple, nothing is accidental and everything holds a meaningful memory.

Mix it up. Immediately to the right as you enter the loft is a small dining table surrounded by metal chairs from Habitat (pink) and Hay (red). The couple are still on the hunt for the perfect dining table, but for the time being this small formica-topped one suits the space well. Behind is a gallery wall hung with everything and anything Ruth and Cory enjoy looking at, from pizza boxes to framed posters.

Bless
This Acid
House.

중요지명피의자 종합공개수배
112
Mehl

Creative screening. Rather than build walls to section off the bedroom, the couple used their clothing rails to screen the space, a clever idea that fulfils two briefs at once. Ruth's rail is a heavy-duty metal one that supports her collection of colourful and eclectic clothing, much of which is vintage. It helps that she has such great taste as the rail is on display from the rest of the loft. Cory's rail is perpendicular to Ruth's (with a drinks cabinet in between, filling the gap). It was constructed from a thick wooden dowel suspended from chain and hooks in the ceiling. Large potted plants add life and colour and fill in the remaining gaps between the bedroom and living-room areas. The pair of birch plywood drawers (below left) is from a collaboration between Zara and Kassl Editions; one of very few new purchases in this home, and solid enough that they will last for years to come.

Q&A

5 minutes with Ruth & Cory.

What's the most important thing for you at home?
Home is my sanctuary, but also a place where we enjoy entertaining so having a peaceful flow and balance through the space is really important.

Do you have a decorating/design philosophy?
When Marie Kondo came along and started talking about only owning things that spark joy, I couldn't understand why this was such a revelation. I try to only bring items into our home that are special, exciting or pleasing. Whether that's a memento from a trip, a handsome piece of furniture or a well-designed device, they should all enrich the experience of being at home.

Do you tend to stay in one property for a long time or do you prefer to move or reinvent your home frequently?
Although I've enjoyed moving around in the past, I now understand this feeling when you've been in a place you really love and get to work on it and make little additions and upgrades over the years as you grow and your tastes change. It develops a lovely richness.

Describe a creative solution to a challenge you faced with your home?
When I moved in, our vinyl collection was living on top of the drinks cabinet and sprawling outwards from there. Cory didn't have a place to store his decks where he could also use them, and I had nowhere to keep my grandmother's old cabinet record player. I built a sideboard that houses the vinyl, integrates the record player and gives the decks a permanent position where Cory can use them whenever he likes. It also doubles as a couch shelf for current reads and mugs of coffee. It's not the most beautiful thing I've ever made, but it works so well that I will remake it at some point with better-quality materials so it's really beautiful as well as exceptionally functional.

Where do you shop for your home? Do you have a favourite shop/source to recommend?
I source a lot from flea markets and *Trödelladen* (junk shops) around Berlin. If there are cardboard boxes to rummage through, I know that I'm in the right place.

What's next for your home?
I would love to redo the kitchen. We cook a lot and it's kind of ridiculous that we've never quite gotten round to it.

Sociable storage. As the kitchen area was short of cabinets, Cory built this island for food prep and to hold kitchen equipment (above and opposite). The stools provide a spot for checking emails on the laptop with a morning coffee, or for dinner guests to perch and chat while the couple cook.

In Heerlen in the south of The Netherlands, Chaggith Stöcker and husband Sotiris Eleftheriou have created a charming and colourful family home in a compact townhouse. Chaggith studied fashion and interior design and dreams of one day owning a homeware shop, Sotiris is a chef in a local Greek restaurant, and daughters Nefely and Anastasia are students. Along with the pets, it is a full house.

At 92 square metres/990 square feet, the home is fairly snug for a family of five, especially with three teenagers and a menagerie of pets (Chaggith plans to add chickens soon), but thanks to careful planning they have made it work. When they bought the house five years ago, after renting for many years, they had to completely renovate and did so on a tight budget, sourcing second-hand and reclaimed items wherever possible. The wall separating the kitchen from the living room was removed to create an open-plan environment. Other renovations were carried out as quickly and economically as possible, so the family could move in and start saving for the rest of the work. However, just when they were about to move, everything went wrong, including the toilet clogging and overflowing and the heating breaking, so for two months they had to stay with a friend – six people and two dogs in one room! All the more reason Chaggith is so grateful for what she calls her dream home.

As an avid collector of vintage, Chaggith decided to leave the walls white, all the better to display her colourful collections and art and make the interior feel more spacious. Reclaimed wooden floorboards were installed everywhere except the hallway, kitchen and bathroom, where cement tiles were laid. From the front door (which Chaggith updated with paint, a vintage letterbox and doorknob, because a new door was too expensive), a small entryway leads both upstairs and into the ground floor living area. This is open-plan, except for a small utility room and a tiny lavatory. Furniture is kept to a minimum – a sofa, small dining table, sideboard, glass-fronted cabinet and vintage wooden unit with drawers for organizing life's many bits and pieces. Almost everything – apart from the sofa, the kitchen cabinets and the locker-style units in the bedrooms – was sourced second-hand. But even the brand-new kitchen feels well loved and lived-in thanks to the irregular pink zellige tiles and concrete work surfaces, which add an air of imperfection that contrasts with the sleek lines of the units.

Upstairs, a hallway leads to three bedrooms and a small bathroom. The two girls share a room while their brother has the smallest room. Due to its limited size, the green-tiled bathroom has an enclosed shower and a lilac vintage sink that was chosen for its joyful colour as well as its neat dimensions. This warm and inviting family home proves that even with a limited space and budget, style doesn't need to be sacrificed when creativity leads the way.

Old and new. Reclaimed floorboards from oudeplank.nl and white-painted walls set a serene stage for Chaggith's vintage glassware and ceramics (opposite). She uses the dining table to photograph her collections to sell on Instagram (@gietemuis) so the family are accustomed to clearing everything away before dinner each night. The ochre velvet sofa is new from HK Living and almost everything else is second-hand.

A compact and joyful townhouse.

WHO *Chaggith Stöcker and Sotiris Eleftheriou, Rëving (18), Nefely (16) and Anastasia (15), dogs Stipje and Coco and pet rabbit Ziggy.*
WHAT *A 1914 townhouse, 92 sq.m/990 sq.ft.*
WHERE *Heerlen, The Netherlands.*

WANDELT
IM
GEIST

WHO *Chaggith Stöcker and Sotiris Eleftheriou, Rëving (18), Nefely (16) and Anastasia (15), dogs Stipje and Coco and pet rabbit Ziggy.*
WHAT *A 1914 townhouse, 92 sq.m/990 sq.ft.*
WHERE *Heerlen, The Netherlands.*

WANDELT
IM
GEIST